RESULTS

The Science-Based Approach
to Better Productivity,
Profitability, and Safety

PRAISE FOR RESULTS

Every leader at Revere goes through John's course and applies the five-step process. The result is a massive change in culture that focuses on relationships, the environment, and implementing this five-step process to achieve results. I'm excited that now we have this "behavioral science bible" to provide to all our leaders to use in their everyday work to drive improvement in their areas.

—Michael O'Shaughnessy, CEO, Revere Copper Products

Dr. John Austin is a premier example of a talk the talk/walk the walk practitioner. This book is the result of years and years for functional, practical and, most importantly, evidence-based, results driven outcomes. John has been the driving force of our nationally acclaimed safety program for over a decade and I can never thank him enough. If results matter to you, this is a must read.

—Steve East, Chairman CSM Group, Proud Recipient of ABC's National Pinnacle Safety Award

Results—everyone wants them and now anyone can achieve them by following the roadmap provided by John Austin. He provides a five-step process to understand and improve performance in organizations while fostering a positive culture built on relationships. His message is practical, understandable, and delivered through a series of relatable stories that reflect those common leadership conundrums that we encounter every day.

—Dr. Linda LeBlanc, BCBA-D, Owner, LeBlanc Behavioral Consulting, Past Editor of *Journal of Applied Behavior Analysis*

I have known John for a few years now and he always motivates me to be the leader I aspire to be. The book is a great read and I am now leaning into the five steps to address some of my areas for improvement.

—Paul Hendry, Global Vice President—Health, Safety and Environment, Jacobs

This book is the Goldilocks of workplace performance books—that is, John Austin gets it just right. The strategies are simple and immediately applicable to workplace settings. Nothing is sugar coated, nor do you feel like you were hit with a hammer or shamed for not getting it right with your employees. The stories, ideas, guidance, and practical activities result in repeated "ah-ha" and "it's so simple, why did I not think of that?" moments. No matter if you are new to managing others, mid-career, or an experienced supervisor or manager, everyone will learn something from the straightforward five-step process for improving workplace relationships, culture, and outcomes.

—Dr. Tyra Sellers, JD, BCBA-D, Owner, TP Sellers, LLC

I have used these tools and can tell you they work. This book provides the tools for anyone to be successful improving results: it's especially helpful to any leader who is trying to get people to do something different. The key is to ensure your people have the time to use these tools to progress, instead of all the time they will otherwise spend going in circles.

—Timothy Rosbrook, Senior VP Human Resources and Organizational Effectiveness, Revere Copper Products

Over the past twenty-five years, I've had the privilege to lead across different industries like education, behavior analysis, and sports. During that time, I made a lot of mistakes. Especially during my earlier years. Why? Well, I believe some key reasons were that I didn't have a model or a mentor, and I was initially exposed to mostly leadership theory primarily focused on traits in my coursework. Sure, the coursework possessed good concepts and provided sound strategies. But leadership is not about traits, concepts, and strategies. It is about behavior. The behavior of the leader and the behavior of those following. And behavior is dimensional.

As a servant leader, I deliberately searched for the impact of my behavior on others. This helped to shape me. But learning on the leadership job, so to speak, is not efficient. And, though well-intended, it came at a cost to those I led, as well as to myself. Oh, how I wish I had this book as I began and refined my leadership journey. In it, John doesn't just tell you the what and the how. Through his practical five-step process, he also gives you the why, the when, the where, the how much, and the how often through compelling stories that illustrate key concepts. And here is the best part. The five-step process isn't just John's way of doing things. His entire approach, laid out in an easy-to-understand format, is grounded in the science of human behavior. This is a must-read for both emerging and veteran leaders.

—Dr. Paul "Paulie" Gavoni, *Wall Street Journal* and *USA Today Best-selling Author*

Dr. John Austin has written a succinct, easy to consume five-step practical guide for leaders striving to "do better." As always, John combines his extensive experience, evidence-based practices, and engaging storytelling to teach leaders how to maximize results. This book is a must read for new leaders, those who wish to start a business, or are interested in improving workplace outcomes. Alignment amongst teams is critical and this book provides simple tools, activities, and tips to do just that!

—Ivy Chong, PhD, BCBA-D, Senior Vice President, Children's Services, The May Institute

I have been using John's approach for almost fifteen years and I have seen it work hundreds of times at our Plant. I still have these five steps on a white board in my office to remind me daily of this approach. This book succinctly delivers the five steps and the personal anecdotes add context and enjoyment. Read the book and start a project—you'll thank John!

—Niall McConville, Site Director, SABIC Mt Vernon, Indiana

I've had the pleasure to work closely with Dr. John Austin since 2021 and all our leaders at CSM Group go through John's Behavior Safety Leadership (BSL) program.

I personally had the opportunity to complete John's BSL course in 2022 and it made a profound impact on me, and I use the five-step process frequently both personally at home and professionally to change behaviors and achieve better outcomes.

Thank you, John, for putting this five-step process together into a guidebook. Will be a great read for all who want to learn and practice the science, and improve their daily lives.

—Stuart Mason, CEO, CSM Group

I believe the difference between successful and unsuccessful leaders is their ability to engage their workforce: articulating their vision, building and aligning your team around a vision, and relentlessly executing to that vision. Dr. Austin nails it. In this riveting, accessible read, Dr. Austin's five-step Behavior Change process helps you set the right environment for your team to succeed. His advice is not an ephemeral "bag of tricks" . . . it's the actionable work (backed by research and his decades of experience) that you need to put in to build the organization and teams that you always wanted to lead. Are you interested self-actualizing as a leader? Pick up this book and start implementing the five steps today.

—Jonathan Mueller, Host of "Building Better Businesses in ABA" Podcast, CEO of Element RCM, and Co-founder of Ascend Behavior Partners

Psychological Safety, Organizational Performance, Organizational Resilience, Systems Safety, and similar themes have become familiar terms in the broader conversation about the workplace.

It's not uncommon to see these concepts discussed on the nightly news, in major newspapers, or on social media. There is a plethora of information relating to organizational factors and systems and others that focus primarily on behavior. There are few, if any, that touch on both. John Austin's book adds much needed context that spans both organizational and behavioral aspects of work, and provides an evidence-based framework leaders can use to successfully navigate the day-to-day challenges in operating a business.

—Brian Hanlon, CIH, CPE, CSP, Director of Environmental Health and Safety, Staples Connect

Having the opportunity to review the draft for Dr. John's "Results" I was drawn back to experiences learning and using the techniques Dr. John shares in the book. One of the most important things I remember is to make sure you are not the reason the environment is not achieving the results you desire.

—Kevin Kirk, CSP, Owner, K Squared Safety

I am lucky to have learned these five steps directly from Dr. John. This book is the roadmap that you need to help you create the right environment for your team. Once you start to understand the importance of this behavioral approach you will start to see better results in safety, quality, and production. If you have problems to deal with that involve people, this is the place to start.

—Bob George, Manager Organizational Effectiveness, Revere Copper Products, Inc.

RESULTS

The Science-Based Approach to Better Productivity, Profitability, and Safety

John Austin, PhD

Printed in the United States of America

Published in Hellertown, PA

Cover and interior design by Christina Gaugler

Hardcover ISBN: 979-8-9879781-0-8

Paperback ISBN: 979-8-9879781-1-5

eBook ISBN: 979-8-9879781-2-2

For more information or to place bulk orders, contact the author at www.drjohnaustin.com.

"The way positive reinforcement is carried out is more important than the amount."

-BF Skinner

*For my mother, who created the right environment
for me to be curious, to always learn, and to share
the learning with others
For my partner, Allison, who always shows up
with thoughtful integrity and a deep heart
For our son, Michael, who makes us so happy*

ADDITIONAL RESOURCES TO SUPPORT YOU!

Download the *RESULTS* Toolkit and your FREE AUDIOBOOK

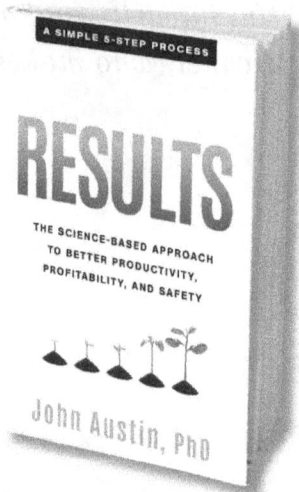

READ THIS FIRST

Just to say thank you for reading my book, I want to share the *RESULTS* Toolkit, at no cost.

It's my gift to you.

GO TO:
**www.reachingresults.com/
results-toolkit**

TABLE OF CONTENTS

PREFACE

Growing up in Baltimore, I was surrounded by hard-working people whom I loved and who loved their families. These were blue-collar, high school–educated people. They worked for people who were at times abusive, mean-spirited, and often put their workers into physically and psychologically unsafe environments. My mom waitressed at a diner early morning and bartended late into the night, working three jobs to support my brother and me. My uncle rose at three a.m. for the frontlines at the gas and electric company. My brother, a Marine, labored in construction and eventually worked his way nearly to the top of a large water supplier. At fourteen I worked in an industrial cleaning plant—not a particularly safe place (physically or psychologically) to work. Getting hurt was part of the job every day and I had to work hard. I saw the lengths my mom and extended family went to put food on the table, and I experienced how stressful it was for the whole family.

Much later, I learned from Dr. Ryan Olson that workers who experience a lack of control and high demands at work have twice the risk of coronary heart disease, acute gastrointestinal problems, and insomnia.[1] Of course, anyone who works in tough manual labor jobs already knows all of this, and my family experienced it too. While I was growing up I experienced life from the hourly worker's perspective. The desire to make work and life better for working people led me to this field, and my background had a big impact on how I approach the topics in this book.

As the first person in my family to go to college, I had *no idea* what to expect. I was repeatedly reminded by my family that they *worked* for a living. And while they were proud of me, what practical things was I really learning? And then I took a course in applied behavior analysis. That changed everything. I learned how to use behavioral science to improve people's lives. This evidence-based science of behavior was exactly what I had been looking for. I caught the behavioral psychology bug, and pursued graduate school, where I learned how these techniques could be applied to any behavior, in any situation, to produce remarkable results. As a university professor I had the privilege of introducing thousands of students to the world of behavioral psychology and guiding them to apply elements of the science into real-world practice.

Over the last thirty years, I've seen firsthand the impact of this work. I've coached thousands of successful projects and published nearly one hundred articles demonstrating the results. Through my consulting business, I have taught thousands of leaders in nineteen countries from ten industries to successfully apply my behavior change process to improve productivity, quality, safety, and culture within their organizations. In many cases lives were saved.

My mission is to help people like my family work in more productive, happier, more motivating, safer, and healthier environments so that they can improve their lives. Most of us spend the majority of our waking lives at work. I have learned that behavioral science can make a difference for anyone. I work primarily with leaders because we know that when leaders embrace and model the practices, the impact is exponentially greater for everyone in the organization—including the leaders themselves.

What environment do you want to work in? If you could improve your life, your family's life, and the lives of your employees, wouldn't you do it? This book is designed to help you do just that.

CHAPTER 1

Success Stories

Your organization is perfectly designed to get the results you are getting right now. Some of this "design" was intentional and strategic and some was unintentional. Either way, you get your current outputs because of your current inputs. Therefore, the only way to get better results is to start doing something new and different. These are simply logical truths.

Behavioral science tells us that leaders who want different results in quality, productivity, revenues, profits, safety, or any other area must create the right environment for the right behaviors to occur. In this book, I will teach you an evidence-based five-step *Behavior Change Process* that can help you get the right behaviors to occur. This process has evolved over twenty-five years from my teaching in business, in industry, and at universities.

I have purposely tried to keep this simple, to make it easier to read and easier to apply.

- **Making it simple means making it accessible.** I use stories throughout the book to make my points. I hope they are familiar enough that you see yourself or people you know in some of the stories.

- **Making it simple means making it useful.** This book is focused on how to apply the science of behavior at work. I will ask you to follow along, complete some exercises, and apply these concepts to something at work while reading the book. You will learn more if you try out some of the things I ask you to do.

- **Making it simple means leaving detail out.** If you want deeper scientific reading on this topic, I give you many options. They are listed in the endnotes and not in the book.

Unfortunately, making it simple does not always make it easy. Doing something new is rarely easy. However, reading this book and following the five-step Behavior Change Process I describe will get you doing new things right away.

A big part of using the tools described in this book involves having dialogue with people and asking the right questions to understand the causes of their behavior before reacting. Many of our challenges with people come from our misunderstanding of why people do what they do. This book tells you how to use the science of human behavior to correct our misunderstandings and create a more effective organization.

ABC Agency[1] was a medium-sized company in the human services and healthcare industry, and they had some major challenges. The quality of their services was not good, so they weren't getting the outcomes they wanted for their clients. This meant that they were not helping children to succeed in and to learn crucial social and communication skills and not helping their parents to manage sometimes challenging behavior from their children.

It was hard to find qualified clinicians, and most left within the first three months. People would joke that all the leaders ran around as if their hair were on fire, all the time. Clients were not improving and were unhappy with their services. Leaders were double- and triple-booked for meetings and had no time to think. We calculated that if the senior leadership team had all their meetings in a row, they would spend about nine months out of the year in meetings, leaving only three months for the rest of their work. It is no wonder that they felt constantly interrupted during meetings and that they needed to reply to emails and instant messages within minutes of them being sent. They were stressed.

Since they were too busy, leaders rarely got input from employees, or even talked to them. Leaders were forced to make big decisions quickly and in a vacuum. Employees didn't feel part of a team, they felt overworked, and they often felt ridiculed when they offered ideas or asked questions. No one had any time for anything but corrective feedback, and a number of employees told me they rarely heard anything good about their hard work. It was draining and depressing.

Immediate improvements started to occur during their Reaching Results leadership courses, and after a couple of years of hard work, ABC Agency is an employer of choice. They deliver high-quality clinical services that get great results for their clients and have a great track record for attracting and retaining people. The reason people love to work there is how everyone treats each other. Leaders recognize that the whole person comes to work, and team members feel like their supervisors really care about them as a person. They call this "positive accountability."

Expectations are clear and agreed on by everyone involved. You can hear specific praise delivered by leaders in virtually every meeting, and although people still don't like to attend so many meetings, they are energized by the interactions with their teammates and feel rewarded for their hard work. People work in a very focused manner and plan for time to think before acting or making big decisions. Employees report feeling a real sense of inclusion and belonging. It is a place where people feel they can say what is on their minds, contribute their best ideas, and be themselves. The CEO of the organization shared with me that people complete their work ahead of time, come to meetings prepared, work together well, and share information. Things are going well, really well.

Baldimore Industries was a highly profitable manufacturing company with a global reach, with most facilities in North and South America. They were making a lot of money, but their injury rate was much higher than they wanted, their costs were high, planning was often poorly executed, and they were missing their quality targets. Leaders were promoted for being "tough and demanding." I attended a senior leadership meeting that started late and ran long, and where people frequently "talked over" another person. They just held their palm up in the speaker's face and raised their voice to talk louder than the person who had the floor. I couldn't believe it.

Micromanagement was rampant. At all hours, senior leaders monitored operations run by people who were three levels down from them and routinely called frontline operators to ask why things were moving too slowly or yell at them over errors in judgment. As a result, of course middle managers and supervisors felt disempowered because they were routinely second-guessed and not allowed to make decisions without permission. Decision-making was very slow and mistakes were not allowed.

Employees rarely spoke up during meetings and almost never shared ideas. At one point, they could not fill a supervisory position for a year because everyone believed they would be fired for making a mistake, as the previous supervisors had been (or so went the rumors). Leaders were so busy that people reported not speaking to their direct supervisor for months at a time and one-on-one sessions, even some of my coaching sessions, were missed without explanation.

They saw improvement within three months of learning behavioral skills in our leadership course. Four years later, Baldimore Industries is proud to be one of the top performers in the world in terms of safety and environmental results. This is a big deal. In their very hazardous markets, many of their competitors measured safety in terms of fatalities and environmental performance in numbers of deadly chemical releases.

An interesting fact is that at Baldimore Industries, *it is safer to work in their manufacturing plants than in their offices.* They have advanced to measuring precursors of injuries because injuries are so infrequent. Their positive results are not limited to safety. Their products are high quality, they have measurably improved their yield, and production is better than ever. The work environment is highly engaging, people are well paid, and it is hard to get a job there.

Frontline workers, executives, and everyone in between report that work expectations are crystal clear and realistic. There are robust feedback exchanges between people. They are very good at finding high-value behavioral measures to track, feed back, and adjust, rather than waiting until the results occur. Finally, most of their leaders were known to be excellent listeners. Sure, they have lots of demanding and results-oriented people, but they place a very high premium on asking questions, listening, and serving their team.

How did these companies get from where they were to where they are now? That is what this book is about. In this book, you will learn how to produce results like the ones described above in the success cases and many other stories I will share. In each case, the organizations and leaders achieved the results by using a reliable and simple process that has worked in over 90% of the 10,000 projects my teams and I have coached. It is *simple* and *effective*, but most people would not say it is *easy*. You will have to do some things that you may not have done in the past to make this work for you.

Of course, the organizations in the success cases and throughout this book are doing lots of things right and much of that is beyond the scope of the Behavior Change Process. This is not a cure-all. However, where most organizations fail is *in the execution of their plans*, and that is what the Behavior Change Process does best. It helps leaders to focus on and measurably improve the vital behaviors needed to deliver results in any area of the business.

The reason these strategies have been so successful is because our process gives leaders a coherent, science-based model of behavior to help them think about, understand, and address the causes of the human challenges they face at work and at home. Perhaps most importantly, the Behavior Change Process described in this book helps leaders to create the right environment for this knowledge to be applied to their current challenges.

I will teach you this Behavior Change Process in the following pages. Before we discuss this process, it is important that you understand some of the thinking that will get in the way of your achieving the organizational results you'd like to see so that you can learn to avoid it and do something better.

This faulty assumption gets in the way of leading

To the casual observer the organizations described above may appear to have nothing in common. They were in completely different industries and different sizes and employed a workforce with different levels of education, and one was mostly female whereas the other was mostly male. They were different on so many levels. And yet, even with all their differences, their leaders failed in similar ways because they did not understand human behavior. In both cases:

- They had too many processes that were often too complicated.
- Expectations were usually vague, leading to inconsistent performance.
- Leaders issued directions that sometimes felt like "orders" to the workforce.
- Leaders measured results, but rarely monitored the actions that produced them.
- Leaders rarely followed up to see the impact of their decisions.
- Threat was routinely used to get things done.
- Individuals were blamed when things went wrong.
- Leaders attempted to motivate by procedure and policy.

Let's get something clear. This is not an indictment of the leaders in these organizations. In both "before" and "after" examples, the leaders' behavior was driven by the environment in the organization. Both organizations had smart and capable leaders who were trying to do the right thing; they had spent lots of time creating a strategy and had many processes, procedures, and policies designed to create a great work environment, and some of the things they were doing were working. They just knew they could do better. It often felt like they were barely holding things together and there was no coherent way of thinking to help their leaders and coworkers be more consistent. The strategies their leaders were using often were ineffective and often only worked in the short term, or had negative future effects because they operated on false assumptions about how humans work.

The primary assumption that is at the heart of many of these problems above is the belief that **telling someone what to do will get them to do it**. This is not true. *Understanding* represents only part of the solution in most cases. The manager who gives an employee a list of expectations only to find that the employee does something else gets frustrated. We see a similar result when workers fail to follow procedures that are clearly documented, click on spammy email links even after completing security training, fail to complete meeting action items even though they are clearly written down and reminders sent, make the wrong product even though the right product is clearly listed on the orders, use the wrong tool when the correct tool is available, or don't do part of their job even though it is clearly listed in their job description. I'm sure you have seen these and other examples in your own job many times, from leaders, coworkers, clients, and maybe yourself.

The primary assumption that is at the heart of many of these problems above is the belief that *telling someone what to do will get them to do it*. This is not true.

This idea that *understanding and telling are not enough* to motivate the person to do the right thing also occurs outside of work in our personal lives, and none of us is immune to this. If you have children, you have been through the "It's time for bed" routine and you quickly learn that simply saying it does not make it happen. Other parenting examples include completing chores, gaming time limits for your children, and healthy eating choices. The same is true for your partner's behavior—telling someone what to get at the store, which sometimes results in a surprise when you get home, planning discussions, budgeting agreements, and even date nights are sometimes forgotten or ineffective at getting the behavior to occur at the right time.

It happens in your everyday life because it is a condition of the world. Think of the local highway for which you know the speed limit. Have you ever exceeded that limit? Why in the world would you do this if you knew the limit? Would more training on following the speed limit help you? Or perhaps a scary video of car crashes? Maybe it would change your behavior in the short term but probably not for long.

The same goes for other things in our lives. Do you always get the recommended amount of exercise, drink the recommended amount of **Just because you know it does not mean you will do it when the time is right.** water, or eat the right foods? Of course, most people don't do all these things consistently, and that is because *a lack of knowledge, awareness, or understanding* is not the problem. My colleagues and I, all of whom teach behavior change, as well as other behavioral experts I know, still struggle with many of these exact examples. *Just because you know it does not mean you will do it when the time is right.*

The leaders in the above examples were in the same situation. They were well meaning, smart, and hardworking like you and me. It's not about blaming them, or you, or me. It is simply that the approaches we develop sometimes do not work because they are a result of *the assumption that knowing generates doing.* We write processes and procedures, develop training, create strategic plans, and explain to people what to do.

When people don't do as instructed, then we get more

direct in our requests, we sometimes issue threats or other
actions out of frustration, and perhaps we even terminate
people who couldn't manage to follow the processes we've
laid out. In fact, this is so common in heavy industry that
safety leaders have a saying about the sorry state of leadership practices that occur after an injury: we tend to blame,
shame, and retrain (none of which works very well).

I have asked thousands of leaders over the years about
what frustrates them most when it comes to leading people at work, and the most common response is that *people
don't do what they are supposed to do.* If knowing something
means we'll do it, then being frustrated with or blaming the
person who failed to follow our
directions would be a logical
response. "I gave them clear
instructions. I can't understand
why they don't do what they're supposed to do!" We all experience it; it's a human condition. In fact, the idea of blaming
someone for their mistakes is so common that psychologists
have studied it and named it the *fundamental attribution
error.* Understanding some of the natural biases and the real
causes of behavior can help us to improve.

**Psychologists call what
people say and do *behavior.***

Drivers of behavior

In most cases, if a person makes an error or mistake it is a
result of the context, situation, or system they are operating
in, not because of their personal characteristics. There is a
more useful way to think about why people do what they
do that reduces our frustration and opens us up to a whole
world of more effective solutions.

If we take the last one hundred years of psychological
research and summarize it, we come away with three factors that cause us to do what we do. We call them the three
drivers of behavior:

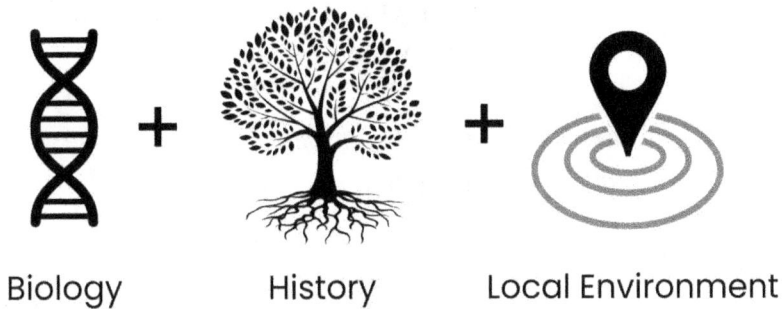

Biology   History   Local Environment

Our DNA or Biology

Our physical makeup undeniably impacts what we say and do at any given moment.

Our History

Everything we have experienced up until this point, all the learning, successes, failures, relationships, and everything our bodies have been exposed to, partly determines what we are likely to say or do next.

Our Environment

What is around us right now partly determines what we will say or do. This includes the physical environment such as room arrangement, tools, computers, desks, lighting, and temperature but also the social environment, such as people and your relationships with them. Your behavior is driven by the environment, but you can also change the environment and that may produce new behaviors from you and anyone else in that environment.

One surprising thing about these three *drivers of behavior* is that you can only control *one* of them. The environment is the only thing we can impact, and this means we can change the environment to change what we say and do. Creating the right environment is the key to improving results at work, and how to do this is the focus of thousands of books and virtually the entire field of behavioral science.

"I don't want to be a product of my environment. I want my environment to be a product of me."

—Frank Costello in *The Departed*

Thousands of studies in psychology are focused on the different ways we can change the environment to get a change in behavior. Changing the environment is the only way to change behavior.

Drivers of results

We have all heard the saying that if you keep doing what you've been doing, you will keep getting the results you've gotten. Another way to think about this is that your organization is perfectly tuned up to get the results you are getting right now. If you accept these premises, then it follows that the only way to get different results is for you and others to start doing something new and different.

This all ties into work results (and results in your personal life) and leadership because the way results are achieved is through the actions (i.e., behaviors) of people. Therefore, we say that behavior drives results. The science of behavior tells us that environment drives behavior. Everyone in the environment helps to create it. However, leaders and managers have more power and influence over the work environment than others do, so we focus mostly on *leader behavior* during this book.

This means in order to get the results you want in quality, productivity, revenues, profits, safety, or anything else, leaders have to create the right environment for the right behaviors to happen. The Behavior Change Process described in this book is an evidence-based way to do that.

Many people ask: Is it even possible to change behavior?

The answer is a resounding "yes"—there are legions of studies showing that people can change their behavior and habits, and we know the conditions under which they will be most likely to change, too. We will cover these topics and give specifics on what you can do to change your behavior and encourage others to change their behavior too.

In this book, I will teach you a five-step Behavior Change Process useful for changing any behavior at work. It does not matter if the behavior is called a "performance problem," "an opportunity," a "good" behavior, or a "bad" behavior. It is all behavior and we don't need to judge it in order to understand it. The model is based on the science of human behavior and so, along the way, understanding the model will help you to begin to get a true understanding of why people do what they do.

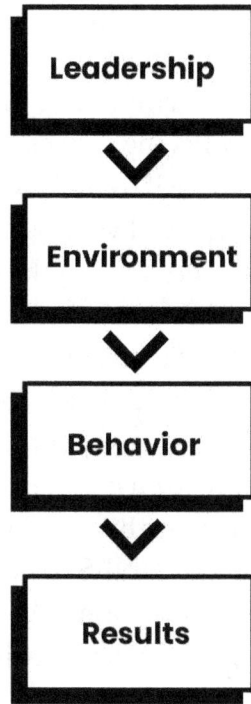

"There is a difference between knowing the path and walking the path."

—Morpheus

The best way for you to learn this approach is to read the book chapters in the order they are presented and apply the steps described in the chapters to an actual performance problem in your organization. If you can't find one at work, then perhaps you can find one at home. Many of my former students found ways to use these techniques at home with their children. I'm not asking you to blindly trust that this works the way I say it does. Instead, experiment and try it for yourself to make your own mind up, but you must follow the steps as I've described if you hope for them to work. Simply understanding the steps but not applying them will *not* work.

My course on these techniques is called Behavioral Science for Leaders, and when it is applied to occupational safety, it is called Behavioral Safety Leadership. Over the last twenty-five years I've taught thousands of leaders in nineteen countries how to use the Behavior Change Process (the five-step process in this book) and leverage the insights from learning Behavioral Science for Leaders to improve results in their organizations. My teams and I have coached over 10,000 improvement projects using these steps and I can tell you that the projects produce measurable results more than 90% of the time.

The science of behavior works 100% of the time. These are *laws* of behavior; they work reliably like gravity works reliably. When the projects don't deliver expected improvements, it is usually because the leader experienced a barrier to implementation. We've seen results improve in productivity, quality, safety, timeliness, profitability, innovation, and just about any area of organizational performance you can imagine.

This five-step Behavior Change Process evolved from years of testing, input, feedback from my students, research as a university professor, clients I have worked with as a consultant, and all that I have learned from many behavioral experts and mentors over the years. The result is a compilation of evidence-based strategies to change behavior. I know they work because they have been tested thousands of times.

Within three months of learning in my course, these techniques are being effectively used by people who had no prior experience in behavior change and even no prior experience as a leader or manager![2]

You might be a leader or individual contributor in manufacturing, construction, healthcare, human services, aviation, utilities, education, transportation, food service, retail, or some other industry. This process has worked in all those industries and more. This might sound too good to be true, but Behavioral Science for Leaders[3] gives us ways to understand and interact with human behavior in any setting. We bring behavioral science expertise, and the leaders inside of those organizations bring their industry expertise. When you can combine industry expertise and Behavioral Science for Leaders techniques, you get powerful insights into how to create the right environment for your people to deliver world-class results.

My "why" is to help people like you learn what we often call the best-kept secret in the world: how to reliably change behavior. To get started, I suggest that you make a list of things that you'd like yourself or your teams to accomplish in your organization. Think about which one you'd like to dive into first. Chapter 2 will give you a brief overview of the five-step Behavior Change Process. In chapter 3 you will select a target and begin your improvement journey. Chapters 4 through 7 will help you to make a change in the target you select. Chapter 8 will give you some ideas on how to create a strong foundation for improvement efforts to work, and chapter 9 gives you some ideas about how to sustain the improvements.

Doing something like applying the concepts in this book is hard. When I am doing something that is difficult, it sometimes helps me to remind myself that "I am doing it for

Future John." Likewise, when I make choices that feel good in the moment but are not good for me in the long run, I might think that "I am doing a number on Future John." This book is about helping you to create a better future for your team and in your business. If you can thoughtfully apply the steps and some of the advice in this book, you will be doing something good for your Future Self!

SOME TERMS USED IN THIS BOOK

Here are some of the terms I use in this book.

ABA: Applied Behavior Analysis. The science of behavior applied to behavior change. It is also the name of an effective therapy based on the science of behavior for people with autism and other disabilities.

OBM: Organizational Behavior Management. The science of applying behavioral principles to change behavior and results in organizations. It is a subdiscipline of ABA.

Positive Reinforcement: Anything that follows a behavior that increases the chances of the behavior occurring again.

Punishment: Anything that follows behavior and decreases the chances of the behavior occurring again.

Behavioral Science for Leaders (BSL): The name of the general approach to leadership described in this book. Also the name of my course to teach leaders to improve results using behavioral science techniques. The five-step Behavior Change Process is a part of it, and the course also includes other skills for leaders, some of which are covered in this book.

Behavior Change Process: a five-step process I teach in my BSL course, and the focus of this book. The process helps you find a key result or behavior and produce a measurable improvement.

Your Behavioral Leadership Project—The Start

Download a fillable PDF of this worksheet at
www.reachingresults.com/results-toolkit

It will help you learn this approach if you consider something at
work that you'd like to focus on improving and carry that focus
through the entire book. I will provide you space for writing about it
in each chapter. Here are some prompts that people often find useful to considering what you could choose to focus on for a project.

Results

List the most important results for you, your team, or your organization here. These might include improving measures of productivity,
safety, quality, revenues, or profitability. If you are struggling with
this question, consider what you are accountable for in your job or
key results named in your strategic plan.

_____

_____

_____

_____

Which of these is most important to improve, right now, in your
organization?

_____

_____

_____

_____

Which of these seems easiest to improve right now?

_____

_____

_____

If you were to improve it by 15%, which of these results would deliver the most value to the team, department, or organization?

_____

_____

_____

Which result will you choose to focus on improving?

_____

_____

_____

CHAPTER 2

The Behavior Change Process

Successful Communication

A medium-sized construction company ran a company-wide survey about twice a year to get feedback and discover where they could improve their culture. Virtually every year, the survey told them that communication throughout the business was a frustration for people. They tried publishing a newsletter, creating videos direct from the founder, broadcasting an internal company podcast and posting things on the wall, and they even developed an app to share information more quickly with everyone in the business. None of these efforts seemed to work. Coworkers felt like they heard about changes through the rumor mill, and they wanted to hear about important things from their direct supervisor.

While taking a course in Behavioral Science for Leaders, the senior leadership team decided they would improve communication once and for all. The problem was leaders and managers were not speaking to their team members to directly share messages with them. They found an easy way to collect data on this, to see if their solutions worked or not. The senior leaders agreed on a message they would share in the coming week to their direct reports, and they would ask those managers to share to their team members too, until it reached everyone in the organization.

Then we called a sizable sample of people across the business and asked if they had heard the message from their manager. A disappointing 5% said they had heard the message! Two weeks later, when we gave them the feedback, the team was discouraged but resolute that they would fix this problem, so we tried again. They wanted a chance to try a new way of getting the message through.

The next measurement showed that 25% of people reported hearing the message. The one after that was 50%, then 75%, then finally after ten weeks of trying new approaches to delivering the messages, they reached 100% of people in the organization. At each improved result, the team congratulated each other and enjoyed the success for a few minutes, talking to each other about how they did it.

Today, years later, this organization still uses a phone tree and measurement to disseminate information and take the pulse of the organization. Each senior leader is assigned a list of people across the organization to call and have a discussion with, answer questions for, get direct feedback from, or share new information with. Obviously, there are other ways to address communication failures, but this organization created one that worked for them. Not surprisingly, when I ask leaders in my course what their organization is not good at, "communication" is near the top of the list every time.

The Five-Step Behavior Change Process

The success stories throughout this book are a product of the five-step Behavior Change Process. This process is the result of twenty-five years of tweaking and feedback from hundreds of clients in a variety of industries; from leaders, managers, and individual contributors; and from—people like you. It has also benefited from the feedback and coaching my team and I did for hundreds of undergraduate and graduate students who took my courses and used the process to create change in organizations. Executing the five steps in this process and learning about the science behind them helps leaders and managers to avoid the errors that the leaders of ABC and Baldimore from chapter 1 made before they understood the drivers of behavior.

We stand on the shoulders of giants to do what we do today. In this book, I will try to attribute the ideas to their rightful owners along the way, but some of the ideas are so fluent in my verbal behavior and so long-standing for me that it is hard to remember exactly where they came from. Attribution does not reduce the value of our work; it brings more gratitude and helps build community.[1]

I am admittedly biased toward the model we will use in this book, as it is the basis for the over 10,000 business improvement projects I have coached as a teacher, consultant, or team leader, with colleagues directly overseeing the projects, and we have data to show that it works. Of those projects, I estimate that when the leader or student follows the steps, they succeed in producing a measurable improvement in over 90% of cases.[2]

When people have difficulty implementing the steps, it is usually because they fail to deliver feedback and recognition. This is why I stress the importance of developing a relationship with the people you hope to influence, because if you can't talk to them, then you can't deliver feedback and recognition in a helpful way either. Even when leaders do have strong relationships with their coworkers, they report that giving feedback and praise is difficult and something they often have the urge to avoid.

When people have difficulty implementing the steps, it is usually because they fail to deliver feedback and recognition.

For fifteen years I taught a practicum at Western Michigan University, in which mostly undergraduate students with no business experience identified a business and helped them solve a problem using this five-step model.[3] We tried to make the process as simple as possible and to create something that someone with any level of experience could use, with about three months of training. After I left the university to start Reaching Results, I worked with some colleagues to adapt that process so it worked the same way in business. With my three-month Behavioral Science for Leaders course, anyone in your organization can learn to apply the concepts in this book and produce measurable improvements, and we have a very high success rate in doing this.[4]

This five-step Behavior Change Process is the centerpiece of the course I teach and it is very flexible. It has been successfully applied at every level of the organization by senior executives and owners, middle managers, and supervisors. It is for people in management roles and individual contributors; for all kinds of results, including productivity, quality, safety, timeliness, communication; and about anything you could imagine. It has also been used to influence large and small groups, and for individualized self-management projects. I will give many examples of each of these throughout the book.

We will review this model as we move through the book, but here is a summary.

Step one: Pinpoint

Decide what behaviors and results you would like to see from yourself or others. Put it in very clearly defined, observable, and measurable terms. Start with one to three behaviors.

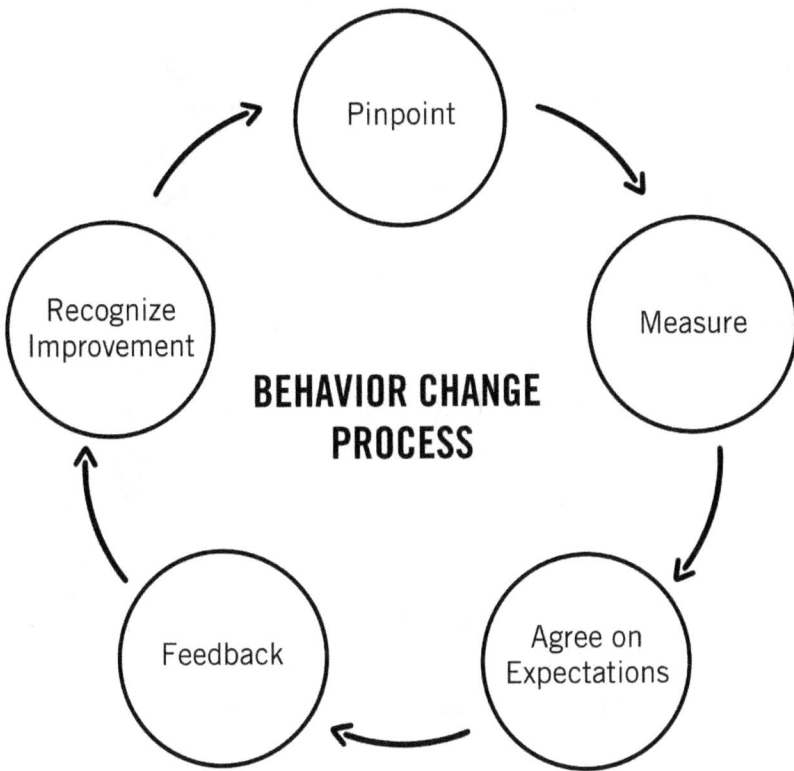

BEHAVIOR CHANGE PROCESS

- Pinpoint
- Measure
- Agree on Expectations
- Feedback
- Recognize Improvement

In the communication example above, the pinpoint was for employees to repeat the message that the senior leaders decided to share. The pinpoint that was required from the leaders was to speak to their teams and share the message within the proper timeframe.

Step two: Measure

Find a simple and quick way to measure the pinpoint, just enough so you know if it is getting better, worse, or staying the same.

In the communication example above, they measured the pinpoint by asking a sample of the company employees if they heard the message.

Step three: Agree on expectations

Have a dialogue with the people whom you hope to help and support using this process. Explain the behaviors you would like to see happen, explain why, ask questions to understand the barriers, and gain a commitment to those behaviors.

In the communication example above, the expectations were created and agreed to by the senior leaders. They were required to discuss expectations with their teams of managers, who also were expected to deliver the message selected by the senior team. They identified and removed barriers to delivering the messages to their teams and this made the behavior more likely to happen.

Step four: Feedback

Deliver feedback regularly on the behaviors being measured so the person knows if things are improving or not.

In the communication example above, feedback was delivered to the senior leaders in the leadership course in the form of the percentage of people who reported hearing their message. They were invited to share that feedback with their teams, too, and this helped them all try different strategies for making sure the message was heard.

Step five: Recognize improvement

Even if the behavior gets better by only 1%, recognizing the behavior will drive it higher and improve your relationships.

In the communication example above, each time there was improvement, recognition and praise were delivered among the senior leaders to each other and also from them to their managerial direct reports.

This is a short summary of the behavior change model, using an example of improving communication throughout an organization. As we will discuss in the coming chapters, effectively applying this process is as much about how you do it and communicate about it as it is about the exact steps you follow.

A Positive Process

I have heard Aubrey Daniels say that performance management (PM) is a "process for positive accountability." I feel the same way about this five-step process. In fact, it seems obvious to me. If you don't use lots of positive reinforcement while doing this, you are missing out on an opportunity. The reason this needs to be discussed at all is that most people who learn behavioral approaches in business have some preconceived notions of what it is and what it is used for. Many leaders enter my courses thinking they will go to set a good example for the others, but this really is for "them, not me." I know that the lightbulb has turned on when they start to say things like, "Now I see I have to change my behavior first."

Many leaders hear about behavior and think, "bad behavior." One senior leader told me before class one day that when he told his peers he was going to learn about behavior management in a course, they said, "Who did you piss off now?" He laughed and said to me, "They have no idea what this course is about!" Others hear the word "consequences" and assume that means negative or aversive consequences. When I explain that this is only part of the story, they often have a hard time getting their heads around the notion that positive consequences can have a mighty impact . . . even larger than negative consequences. The related idea of reinforcing small successive approximations is often also stymying to leaders.

It is useful to discuss what BSL is and what it is not because most people have misconceptions when they start learning about this approach. The way we learn about concepts is to see or hear positive examples and non-examples of it. Psychologists call this concept learning.

Behavioral Science for Leaders (BSL) is NOT about:

- "Fixing" the poor performers or giving someone an "attitude adjustment"
- Blaming, transferring, or terminating people for their mistakes
- Setting expectations and then "getting out of the way"
- Using negative consequences like punishment and discipline or threats
- Coddling people
- Showering people with unearned praise

When we can help leaders change their thinking and approach slightly, to focus on positive elements of performance, their teams are often shocked. Some have even asked, "What did you do with my boss?" They report finding it hard to believe such a change has occurred. It is important to remember that this is not about changing people. All behavior is a product of the environment we operate in—that is true for leaders, their direct reports, you, and me. Yes, change is possible, and change becomes commonplace when using this process because we are using a scientific approach.

Now let's discuss what BSL is. Behavioral Science for Leaders is:

Positive

It is forward-looking rather than focused on the past. It is meant to help, and if correctly done it often feels good to everyone involved. It generally means delivering praise when it is earned and doing so liberally. We are often too stingy with our recognition, for no good reason. People often contrast this with having a "soft touch," suggesting that there is less accountability in a positive approach, but this is not true because the recognition is always earned through productive behavior. Praising good behavior has no downside. People are still accountable to the rules in a positive environment such as this. In fact, there is *more* accountability in a positive environment.

Safe

Everyone should know the expectations and that feedback exchanges are encouraged, and they should be respectful, professional, and helpful. Leaders should convince their teams they are trying to help them, and the leaders need to believe it.

Fair

Since it emphasizes behavior measurement, data, and not judgment, it has the potential to reduce gender, racial, or other biases over more subjective approaches.

Worker-centric

You need them more than they need you. Bringing out the best in your teams is about creating a positive environment for everyone in the organization.

Non-judgmental

This is a no-blame approach that helps you to understand why results and behavior are occurring. Judgment and blame hinder understanding. Understanding why people are acting a certain way improves engagement and results.

For everyone

When clients ask me who should learn this—if they can't include all leaders—they typically want to add the "hard cases" to the course, to see if we can "fix" them. Whereas

I'm always up for a challenge, "fixing someone" is impossible and it's not the goal of this approach. You can help someone change their behavior and support them, but this is different from what many leaders think it is.

A multiplier

Either way, I think focusing on "problem employees" is a poor use of resources for several reasons. Imagine, for instance, you manage a team of salespeople. A few sell $1000 a week and some others sell $100 a week. If you can get a 15% improvement in their performance, which one would make you more money?

The most successful applications of these techniques I have witnessed has been in organizations who decided to teach every person in a managerial or leadership role about behavioral science and to expect them to apply what they have learned to improve the business.

"The What" vs. "The How"

Each of the five steps in the Behavior Change Process have been studied as behavior change techniques and published in studies since the 1960s as part of the science of applied behavior analysis (ABA) and organizational behavior management (OBM). These scientific studies are an excellent source of *what* you could do to change behavior—like a cookbook, they give the recipe for making the prescribed behavior change.

What they don't generally do very well is tell us *how* to deliver the techniques. Think of it as a cookbook that tells you what the ingredients are but leaves out the measurements of each ingredient. In other words, in many of the published studies, the context, the tone of voice, and the necessary conditions needed to make the techniques acceptable to the receivers are all left up to the practitioner to figure out.

For this reason I have worked to find evidence-based recommendations on how to set the stage for behavior change techniques to be most effective or for people to want to use them in the first place. Since I began in this field in the early 1990s, applied psychology has exploded with activity. Hundreds of books have been written on psychological approaches to behavior change, habit building, leadership, parenting, marketing, communication, and myriad other topics. Many of these books and articles describe various ways that we can set the stage for behavior change.

I have built many of the best practices from this wide array of sources into the way we teach Behavioral Science for Leaders because I realized that leaders in my courses needed more instruction and coaching on how to deliver the five steps in the Behavior Change Process. Some of these areas are described below, and I dive deeper into some of them later in the book.

Psychological safety

Psychological safety is the idea that you can say what is on your mind without fear of reprisal from the group. Edmonson's (2018) book, *The Fearless Organization*, is a great review of research, writing, and practice in psychological safety. It is essential for today's leaders to understand this concept, why it is important, and how to promote it among their teams.

Behavioral integrity

Behavioral integrity[5] is the extent to which your team and coworkers believe you do what you say you will do. In applied behavior analysis research, this is often called *say-do correspondence*, but it just hasn't been studied in those terms among leaders. In the broader psychology literature, studies have shown that if coworkers believe you have high behavioral integrity, then *they trust you more, they see you as more competent*, and *they are more likely to go above and beyond* when you make a request. In addition, organizations that practice a culture of behavioral integrity have higher profits.

The psychology of influence

Goldstein and colleagues wrote a great book describing fifty ways to influence behavior, based on social psychology research.[6] Most of the effects are small and considered "nudges"; however, they get you thinking about the various modes of social influence that we don't always consider.

Communication science

Based on the science of communications, we know that "awareness" has little impact on behavior. We know that most emails are not read by their recipients. When they are read, we know that few people understand the tone and sentiment of the message. Despite our knowledge that most written communication does not work as planned and emails are misread for tone, often harming relationships, we still use these techniques more than face to face, live video, or phone communications. Larkin and Larkin wrote an excellent article on this and have published many resources to help us communicate more effectively.[7]

Self-management techniques

There are many resources for self-management, and although essential for leaders to learn, most of these are beyond the scope of this book. One that I will mention here is time management, or as many call it, task management. The key resource in this area is called *The Getting Things Done*

Workbook by Allen and Hall.[8] In the book, they describe a system of managing tasks that is easy and highly effective. It is also the top concern I hear from executives for their own improvement and their team's improvement.

Acceptance and Commitment Therapy (ACT)

ACT is a way of thinking about our own thoughts as separate from us and observable and helping others to make sense of their thoughts. It suggests techniques that can make change initiatives more effective, such as explaining *why* a task is important when setting expectations, and many other techniques, including management of stress and burnout reduction.[9]

The science behind this approach is based in the experimental analysis of behavior (specifically called relational frame theory), but the practice has become a widely used approach that has evolved into its own field. ACT is based largely on the idea of building skills related to psychological flexibility.

Your Behavioral Leadership Project– Setting the Stage

Download a fillable PDF of this worksheet at
www.reachingresults.com/results-toolkit

Below are some questions to reflect on. Sometimes the response
to these questions leads learners toward an improvement project
focus, so try to keep an open mind and be honest with yourself.

Review

What business result from chapter 1 would you like to improve?

_____

_____

_____

_____

_____

Reflect

1. Could you see yourself using the five-step Behavior Change Process? Why or why not? When leaders in your organization lead or manage teams, which of the steps do they most often leave out or struggle with?

_____

_____

_____

_____

2. Do you feel like anything is left out of this five-step process? If so, make a note of it here so you can come back and review your answers after you read about the steps in more detail.

_____

_____

_____

3. Where else could you build these practices from the five steps into your organization?

_____

_____

_____

4. How psychologically safe is your organization? What evidence do you have for your response? Beware of confirmation bias (i.e., we see only what we want to see).

_____

_____

_____

5. How would your team rate your behavioral integrity? Think of each of your direct reports individually. How would you rate their behavioral integrity?

_____

_____

_____

6. What do you think behavioral science is about? Has your opinion changed since starting this book? Why do you want to learn these techniques?

_____

_____

_____

7. Are there opportunities for you and your team to improve their communication skills? What behaviors would you like to see improve?

_____

_____

_____

8. Do you manage your own behavior well? What areas could you improve in? How about for your team members?

_____

_____

_____

CHAPTER 3

Step One: Pinpointing

A senior manager at Optimistic Behavior Change (OBC), a medium-sized human services and healthcare agency, wanted to improve the culture of the organization. They had a problem with turnover. They were finding it hard to attract talent. They had quality problems, and there was plenty of negativity among the staff who delivered services. People complained about communication, they wanted more pay and . . . well, things were not going as well as the leaders of the business had hoped. So they started a focus on culture, because so much seemed wrong in the business.

Most of the leaders in the business were clinicians, so they had not really learned about culture in their degree program, which focused mostly on treating problem behavior among people with disabilities. When it came to leading and managing employees, there was almost nothing taught. They thought this was ironic because the first job that most new graduates are hired to do involves managing teams of people and supervising others in the treatment of problem behavior.

In the applied behavior analysis (ABA) world, that usually means managing frontline caregivers (known as RBTs®, Registered Behavior Technicians®). It's mostly the same in other disciplines outside of ABA, too, including manufacturing, construction, and industry. Even when people are promoted within their organization, they are normally promoted because they are great at their job. So, you're good at your job. You're not necessarily good with people and you might know literally nothing about managing others. And yet, you get a promotion to be a leader, you are handed the title and congratulated, and then you start immediately. No training, no coaching, no real mentoring. That's the norm.

You come across challenges such as those described above, and because you are highly conscientious and responsible, you reach for anything you can find online that might help you improve your organization's culture. And of course you find a multitude of resources on culture and how to improve it. However, none of them are consistent because none are based on a solid scientific approach. Plus, most approaches were short on details and vague in terms of how to implement the change. They seemed like they were just based on the opinions of the writers, which may be okay in some situations, but in this case, you want to be sure that this will work.

Enter Behavioral Science for Leaders. Based on behavioral science, this approach involves applying evidence-based approaches to solve organizational challenges.

Once the leaders at OBC started to learn to practice Behavioral Science for Leaders, they realized that "culture" was far too broad, too hard to define, and too hard to measure to be a good focus of their efforts. In a behavioral view, culture is a broad descriptor of what people in the organization say and do each day. Another way to define it is that culture is the result of what is reinforced and punished in the business.

They learned that the first step in making a change is to get very clear about what you want to see from people. This was a challenge because, as a matter of urgency, the leaders were very focused on what they did not want to see, e.g., they wanted less complaining, less calling in, less negativity, etc. These leaders needed to practice the skill of pinpointing.

The term *pinpointing* might have been coined by Ogden Lindsley as early as the 1950s[1] when he was working in BF Skinner's lab at Harvard. In behavior analysis and in scientific circles it is often called "operationalizing" and **it means to define the behavior in a way that allows for it to be observed and measured.** If you have a background in applied behavior analysis, you probably know something about pinpointing. However, there is a good deal of subtlety in this skill, so no matter what your background is, don't take it for granted. According to Daniels and Bailey,[2] good pinpoints are:

> **Pinpointing means to define a behavior in a way that allows for it to be observed and measured.**

Observable

You can see or hear it happening. Thoughts aren't really included, unless you are monitoring your own thoughts.

Measurable

You can *count* the number of times it happens. People are very used to using ratings at work, but these are far inferior to behaviors and so you should really try to figure out how to count the behavior. Usually when clients insist on ratings, it means they haven't defined the behavior well enough or that they can't directly observe it. Either way, ratings are an approximation at best. Use them as a last resort.

Active

Focus on what you want to see. Don't focus on what is not happening. Framing the pinpoint in a positive manner allows you to focus on the future and not the past and to graph and reinforce improvements rather than correct errors. Correcting errors is less fun for you and *definitely* less fun for the performer! Some examples of active pin-points include: "Coming in to work on time," as opposed to "Not showing up to work" or "Delivering reinforcement within thirty seconds of the target behavior," as opposed to "Not delivering reinforcement in a timely manner."

Reliable

This is a term from applied behavior analysis, which means that two independent observers agree or disagree on whether the pinpoint has occurred or not. Here is the acid test for a reliable pinpoint: If, when you tell them about the pinpoint, you find that someone on the team asks, "What do you mean by that?" then you have not defined it well enough. Go back and add some detail so that everyone knows exactly what you mean when you talk about the pinpoint.

I have taught how to pinpoint more times than I can count, and in nearly every case—even with highly trained behavior analysts—people tend to default to using general terms (we call them "labels") instead of behaviors or pinpoints. Pinpointing usually feels laborious or like "splitting hairs" to the learner, but that's normal. That is exactly how I want them to feel, so leaders start to understand the level of detail necessary to effectively pinpoint. This skill is one of those that is simple to understand and yet it is not easy to implement. It's worth spending some time on this part before progressing through the other steps.

When you are in the process of learning this skill, it's useful to take some broad terms that are commonly used and talk about how to define them. Let's try it below, with the term "culture." There are no right or wrong answers, as long as everything you list meets the defining characteristics of a pinpoint—make sure it's measurable and observable!

When someone in your organization thinks of culture,

what pinpointed behavior might be involved? Write your ideas below:

_____

_____

_____

For each pinpoint you wrote, go back and answer the following two questions:

1. What does it look like when it happens? Describe in detail what you would see if you saw it happening.

2. If you were in a group of ten people, would they all agree that the behavior happened or didn't happen? If there is any disagreement, you will need to define the behavior more specifically.

Some common pinpoints from my clients to improve their teams and culture include:

- Meeting deadlines
- Starting and ending on time
- Praising good work
- Delivering feedback at a ratio of four positives to one corrective, or better
- Managers speaking to each team member every day
- Managers and supervisors asking questions
- People speaking to each other to have dialogue more than email or text
- Simplifying written messages to make them more readable

- Asking people what frustrates them about the work
- Removing barriers to effective working

Some common pinpoints from client leaders to improve their own behavior include:

- Responding to email or calls within forty-eight hours
- Reducing use of email
- Planning in think time each week
- Planning the upcoming week
- Estimating time required for tasks more accurately
- Coaching members of my team
- Engaging my team during meetings
- Asking questions
- Soliciting feedback

This process may not be what you think it is.

When my family got a puppy for our teenager, my wife found all kinds of great behavioral resources to help us learn to manage the puppy's behavior, house-train it, help it to learn to sit, or teach it to ring a bell when it needs to potty outside. This last one was harder for us than the others because our puppy loved to play with the bells! One of my favorite resources was this trainer's advice for dealing with times when the puppy had an "accident" in our house on the floor. He said that when our puppy has an accident or makes a mistake, roll up a newspaper and smack yourself with it! Don't smack the puppy. It's your fault, after all!

When finding a pinpoint, many leaders start by trying to get others to stop doing various things. However, it is often more productive to look at your own behavior and figure out how your behavior might be contributing to the challenge and how you can get a different outcome by doing something differently.

In behavior analysis, there is a famous old saying that "the rat is never wrong," since early research involved rats as subjects. We don't want to compare people to rats, so I prefer the more modern equivalent, "The learner is never wrong." This means that whatever behaviors and results you are getting from your team, department, division, or organization are due to the environment that has been created, not because of some flaw of your employees.

Don't judge the person; just observe the behavior and learn. Treat the behavior as a data point that shows you the results of the environment in your organization. Imagine you were manufacturing a widget, and the widgets were coming out differently than you planned. They were lower quality, didn't adhere to your specs, or whatever. How would you address this discrepancy? Would you go and blame the machine? Would you get a new machine or discipline it? Of course not. You would diagnose the causes of the problem and adjust the machine to improve the parts it produces. In this example, the environment is the machine, and the behavior is what it produces. Treat the behavior as a data point that tells you something about your workplace and what you might need to change to get a better result.

Who creates the environment? Owners, leaders, managers, supervisors, coworkers, and clients do. So, remember, this approach is not about finding the problems and rooting them out. Sure, you can take that approach, but it's far more uplifting to approach this as a chance to build prosocial, inclusive, and productive behaviors. Not only is it more uplifting, but that positive approach brings along lots of other positive benefits, including improving retention, discretionary effort (going above and beyond the basic requirements), relationships and happiness.

Choice

Would you rather choose what to do during your day or be told every detail? To simply follow orders or to think about the best way to do things, especially when conditions change? Which model would you rather your employees follow? Most people who are engaged in their jobs hate to be told what to do in a one-sided way. Instead, they want input or some control into how things are done, and they want to own that part of the job or task, even at home. In fact, there are data to show that people who have low control over their work and few opportunities for advancement are far more likely to suffer from heart disease! There is a lot to say about this topic when it comes to leadership and management, and there is a fine line to walk between giving people control over how or what they do and delivering high-quality results. We will touch on some of these points later.

Olson found that giving someone a choice between relatively equal alternatives improved engagement by 20%. Imagine this . . . just by giving people a choice, we create motivation! It follows that giving people in your organization a choice of which pinpoint they focus on is a great way to earn their engagement with the process. That is why I have always taught it that way in my courses. The moral of this story is to try not to dictate the exact rules and actions but try to give them some choice in the matter.

You may be concerned that if you give them a choice, people will choose the wrong thing to focus on. This may happen, true, but then you can coach. Recall that learning these skills is a shaping process. Shaping is a process of rewarding small steps toward a final goal. That means that the first improvement project you select is simply one among many repetitions. That usually takes the pressure off selecting the perfect pinpoint to focus on improving.

Another strategy is to give people boundaries within which they can select a pinpoint that is meaningful to them or their teams. For instance, you might ask people to select a behavior that could improve retention, leadership, or quality. It is okay for a leader to set an expectation as a label (like quality, safety, or leadership) as long as you help your team to pinpoint what it means and everyone agrees to commit to those well-defined behaviors.

One human services client we worked with[3] asked people to focus on quality, and the topics that leaders selected included, among others:

- accuracy of instructions
- accuracy of reinforcement delivery
- accuracy of error correction
- correct adherence to behavior program checklist items
- on time behavior report completion
- accuracy of data sheet completion

In all cases, leaders were allowed to select the most important quality-related behaviors for their teams and the clients they served. It would have produced a far inferior effect to tell everyone to focus on the same exact pinpoint no matter the needs and motivations of the team and clients, and yet it is far simpler for a leader to mandate a blanket focus in their organization in the name of consistent practices.

Key leader behaviors

What most organizations find as they start this journey of culture change through behavioral science is that there are too many behaviors to focus on and people quickly become overwhelmed. One approach to dealing with this overwhelm, as mentioned above, is to give people boundaries within which they can choose the proper behaviors to focus on for their own local environments. When using this approach, I am partial to helping people to become focused on the key leader behaviors they would like to see.

There are many reasons to focus on leader behaviors, but a very behaviorally sound reason is that leaders have a key role in creating the environment that everyone else in the business is operating in. As we know, the primary driver of behavior is environment, and that is something that effective leaders can curate.

So which leader behaviors are the most effective ones? That's a key that is open for interpretation, but there are some studies on this topic that can guide us. Komaki's work[4] in studying competitive sailing skippers tells us that the leaders whose teams win the most often do a few key things differently from the losers. The winners tended to *set behavioral expectations, frequently monitor* to see if they are happening as planned, and then either *correct or praise execution* by team members.

Many behavioral studies have shown the importance of feedback[5,6] at improving performance, and this is logical too—people need information in order to improve. However, Laraway published an analysis of large data sets on leader behaviors from Qualtrics that provides some interesting subtlety to the existing data.[7] Laraway studied the leader behaviors that most closely correlated to employee engagement and retention. What he found was that the top three leader behaviors are reflected in the following questions:

1. My supervisor gives specific praise when good work is done.
2. My supervisor solicits feedback.
3. My supervisor sets explicit expectations.

The top question that related to retention was, "My supervisor cares about me as a person." Most people are surprised that *giving feedback* is not included in these questions. I think it makes sense because, as we will discuss later in the book, leaders who ask for feedback can give feedback more effectively.

Frustrations

As part of my Behavioral Science for Leaders course, I start off by asking participating leaders what frustrates them at work. They say things like communication, IT systems, laziness, lack of initiative, email, and others. Do any of these sound familiar to you? There is a remarkable consistency across audiences and industries and although people use lots of different words for it, the most consistent frustration has been "Why won't they do what they are supposed to do?" That suggests that many of us are far from earning discretionary effort. We're talking about minimal performance here, not going above and beyond the minimum. Therefore, we must all learn to practice the fundamentals of management and leadership. We don't need anything super fancy until we've gotten the simple stuff right, and you can gain a great deal by getting the simple stuff right.

Later in the course, once I've modeled how to do this, I ask learners to find a team of people in the business (ideally, a team they manage) and ask them, "What frustrates you when it comes to working here?" After they ask the question, they are to take out a notebook and take notes, thanking people for sharing this information with them. It's important that you don't try to explain anything as you get this important feedback, but rather you should simply say, "Thank you." We have found this is a highly effective way of building trust, opening communication by creating a safe space for people to share their thoughts, and, most importantly, it tells you some areas that could be addressed to improve the way the work is done. Pay careful attention during these discussions because you will often hear ideas for pinpoints you could choose to focus on for your Behavioral Leadership Project.

Asking for frustrations is not a practice you'd want to engage in every week, but perhaps once a quarter it could be good to do. The purpose is not to encourage complaining but rather to openly talk about the stuff that gets in the way of happily doing our best work. Think of it this way. If you were the owner of the company, would you want to put people in situations in which they were constantly frustrated by trying to do the right thing for the clients and the business? Of course not. And yet, owners do it every day in every organization I have ever worked with over the past thirty years. Not every frustration is something you can change or remove, but instead of acting like it doesn't exist, just talking about it and being clear that you can't change it, or finding a workaround, is helpful to people.

In most organizations, leaders know which results they would like to see. It is this process of identifying, measuring, agreeing on, delivering feedback on, and recognizing the behaviors, that is most difficult to execute.

Results

The success of your organization depends on results. Every experienced leader knows this. The way to make your pin-pointed behavior most impactful is to link it to some import-ant result in your organization. Find a result that you would like to see improve and then identify the vital few behaviors that will move the needle on your target result. In most organizations, leaders know which results they would like to see. It is this process of identifying, measuring, agreeing on, delivering feedback on, and recognizing the behaviors that is most difficult to execute. That is why the focus of this book is on those steps and not really on how to identify an important result.

This book will be much more valuable to you if you try to apply some of the concepts as you learn them. In the follow-ing pages, I will lead you through a process of discovering what you would like to focus your efforts on improving. Then you will be prompted to develop and implement an action plan to produce the improvements you are looking for.

Your Behavioral Leadership Project–Pinpoint

Download a fillable PDF of this worksheet at
www.reachingresults.com/results-toolkit

Review

What business result from chapter 1 will you focus on improving?

_____

_____

_____

_____

What are the critical few behaviors that are required to achieve this
result? Any or all of these could be the pinpoint focus for your project. Pick something that you can see change within 6–8 weeks. If
it will take longer than this, then pick something different until you
have practiced the entire process a few times.

_____

_____

_____

Foundational pieces in place (mark "Y" for yes or "N" for no):

- ☐ Psychological safety: is it safe for coworkers to say what is on
  their mind?
- ☐ Communication: is communication lean and easy to understand?
- ☐ Behavioral integrity: do I do what I say I will do? Do coworkers?

☐ Self-management: do I manage my own behavior and keep my promises? Do my coworkers?

Reflect

Is there something that would make your life better if you could improve it?

_____

_____

_____

_____

Is there something that would help your team at work if you improved it?

_____

_____

_____

_____

Is there something that would help your clients if you improved it?

_____

_____

_____

Is there something that frustrates you (or your team or their teams or the clients and caregivers) that you could address?

_____

_____

_____

What are some of the key behaviors you would say drive the success of your organization, division, or department? Would improving
any of these be a good use of time?

_____

_____

_____

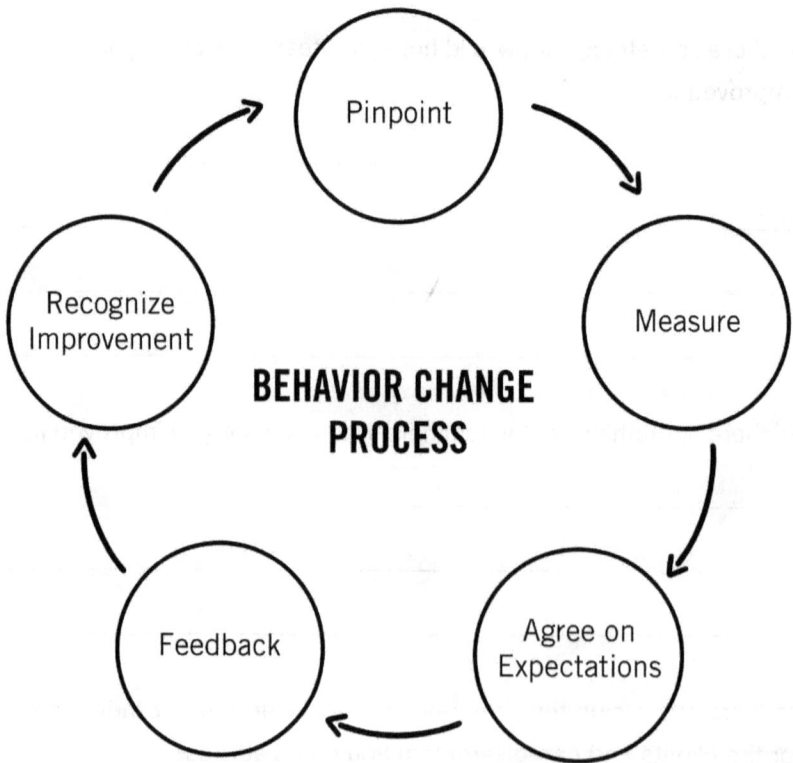

What pinpoint would you like to focus your project on? Pick one thing from the lists above to use as an example in working through the rest of this book. That thing could involve your behavior or someone else's behavior, but if it is something else, be sure that you have a relationship with them and interact with them regularly.

_____

_____

_____

Double-check

How does the pinpoint relate to the result you wanted to improve?

_____

_____

_____

CHAPTER 4

Step Two: Measurement

Evan was a supervisor who spent a lot of his time in meetings and directly observing to see how staff were interacting with clients. While he was taking the Behavioral Science for Leaders class and looking for something he could use as a project, he held a meeting with his team to ask what frustrates them. They shared with him a whole list of complaints, including the parking situation. Due to a current construction project, staff had to walk two blocks to get to the office, and they did not like this at all—especially when it was cold outside. They also felt like there was a lot of negativity on the team and that the only time they ever heard anything from management (this included Evan) was when something was wrong or when a new policy was being rolled out because of someone not complying with existing procedures.

Evan reacted well to this difficult feedback, and afterward he explained that some things are in his power to fix and some are not. The parking situation was not one of them he could fix, but he promised to pass on their frustrations to his manager and see what could be done. The meeting ended, and he promised to go away and think about the rest of the feedback. He was puzzling over how to get the team to "be nicer" to each other and how to get the senior leaders in the company to stop issuing new procedures, and both seemed impossible to him. He can't control how friendly people are to each other, can he? And how in the world could he ever impact someone who is two levels above him in the organizational hierarchy? Plus, although he understood their frustrations, his team needed new and better processes and needed to do a better job following them. He didn't always disagree with the idea of rolling out new ones.

One of the key points that Evan remembered from his Behavioral Science for Leaders class was that you can only have a lasting influence on people with whom you have a relationship. In other words, if you don't regularly interact with them, you can't focus a behavior change project on their behavior. So that meant that, while he could pass on feedback to his manager about the process rollouts, he couldn't really try to influence a team of leaders that his boss reported to. When it came to his team feeling like everything was negative, he realized that he did have some influence over their behavior, because he was part of the daily environment. He realized that their words and actions were things he could see, measure, and possibly even change over time. However, most of the negative things and gossip among the team only got to him through other people—he rarely saw it himself. That made measuring it more complicated.

He considered for a while how to measure gossip and negative talk using surveys and other indirect ways when the idea hit him. He was part of the environment they were operating in too. What he said each day to his team could have a bigger impact than he realized, and in truth he was usually looking for what they were doing wrong. Furthermore, he could control his behavior more easily than trying to focus on other people. Maybe if he changed his behavior, it would have a positive impact on the team? After discussing positive reinforcement in class and how important it was to deliver lots of it—in fact, studies show that high-performing teams have a ratio of 5.6 positives to 1 negative[1]—he realized that whereas he always thanked people, it wasn't specific or thoughtful. It was just polite, and politeness is good but it doesn't really change behavior.

Evan decided that his improvement project pinpoint would be delivering specific praise to a team member when he saw something going well. But how would he measure it? The best measurement systems are simple and just need to tell you if things are getting better, getting worse, or staying the same. He tried using tally marks on a small pad of paper, but he kept losing the pad or forgetting to make a mark when he delivered the praise. So, instead, he made it even simpler.

Every morning at home, he put eight quarters in his right pocket. He wanted to start by delivering praise eight times each day at work. That isn't a huge amount, but it would be eight times more than he was currently doing it! So, each time he delivered praise, he moved one quarter from his right pocket to his left pocket. At the end of the day, before leaving for home, he counted the number of coins in his left pocket and added a data point to his graph.

Most people we work with tend to overcomplicate measurement, and sometimes they forget that data collection is a means to an end. They develop database pivot tables, QR codes, and complex surveys that no one wants to complete. They often look for automated ways to collect the data when there are usually simpler solutions. Measurement does not need to be fancy or "high tech" or even involve technology at all.

The 1990s weren't that long ago (at least in my mind), and for studies we were publishing in a top behavioral science journal, the *Journal of Applied Behavior Analysis* (*JABA*), we were using pencil and paper to record data in notebooks and hand-drawing graphs until the final version. In many industrial applications of OBM published in the research journals starting in the 1960s and into the 1990s, graphic feedback was delivered to employees on a sheet of paper with a hand-drawn graph. So don't let the technological elements of data collection get in the way of observing and collecting simple data.

Use existing data

Over the years, I have seen many other measurement systems, all created by leaders in organizations and participants in my courses. People often forget that there are existing data on elements they would like to improve, and using existing data makes it far easier for you to make an improvement. One leader wanted to increase the number of views their organization was receiving on their posts on YouTube. Another leader wanted to improve their visibility on LinkedIn, so they started posting more frequently and trying new strategies. These are results, of course, and they reflect certain behaviors. Perhaps these are not the sort of behavior changes you imagined when you started reading this book, but they do require new behavior from the individuals running those projects and those they wish to influence, so in my opinion they qualify. Behavioral science can be used anytime there are people involved.

Other examples of people using existing data include:

■ Improving time management by coding calendar appointments as vital (only I can do this), important (I probably should be involved), stop doing, or must delegate

- Using automatically collected insights from your computer, watch, or phone regarding tasks completed, time spent, sleep, steps, and follow-ups completed
- Using data collected by coworkers to show change over time
- Using inspection or observation data that had been previously recorded
- Using existing survey data to understand the people on your teams and opportunities for improvement

Not everything fits the mold

Not everything you'd like to improve is easily counted or even rated. For example, Sheila wanted to improve the organization of her office space. She found that over the years, she had gotten into a habit of piling things on and around her desk. This made it harder to find things she needed but also made it harder to clean her office, and this made it less inviting for her to spend time there. She found herself working in other rooms, and when she had people into her office, she was embarrassed at how messy it had become.

Sheila wanted to focus on cleaning her office for her course project, but she was stuck on the measurement part. How do you measure cleanliness? There actually is a scientific way that involves creating a checklist and recording the percentage of cleaning items completed each day, if you're interested in learning more.[2] However, that is far more than you need in most cases. We try to keep things simple for leaders learning this process.

Sheila decided to measure the cleanliness of her office by taking photos of the critical areas each week. This showed whether she had filed her important papers and whether she kept her organization over time. As she was working on it, she realized that she was sometimes missing the photo and things were slipping. So, she added an element to the solution wherein she engaged her supervisor (with whom she had a great relationship and who was nonjudgmental about the office conditions) and sent her supervisor a photo each week to keep herself honest about the process. It worked amazingly well and helped her rekindle a habit of cleaning and organizing her office. Over time, she was able to stop the photos and the habits persisted because she had created a daily routine and realized that it felt good to have a more organized office. I've also seen leaders use before and after photos to measure housekeeping in construction, distribution centers, and industrial sites.

Don't be afraid to be creative in your measurement strategies—to be sure, counting is the most accurate way to measure, but it is not the only way. The measurement system simply needs to show you if things are getting better, getting worse, or staying the same.

Self-monitoring works

Sometimes you don't have to do the data collection, but you can ask others to tell you what they are doing. If it is simple, quick, and nonthreatening for them to do, this can be an effective practice. There are things to avoid in this practice, however. I have seen leaders who basically assign their project to someone on their team and that person then collects the data, gives the feedback, and so on. This is not a great idea since the whole point is for *you* to have this experience and learn about how it is done through experience. You can't earn experience through delegation.

When self-monitoring works, it is typically because you are trying to influence some behavior that you can't easily observe. It works best when you ask for the data in a way that is safe for the reporting coworker. One way to ensure this is to praise them for collecting and sharing the data—you are trying to reinforce accurate data collection, not improvements. The idea of reinforcing accuracy is that you just want them reporting accurate data so that you can use that to make it obvious to them what their performance looks like.

Once they see what their performance is relative to the goal or expectation, they will often adjust their behavior, or they may let you know how ridiculous your expectation is! If you try to praise improvements in the data, some people will take that as an implicit suggestion to report inflated or inaccurate data. Since you can't see the behavior happening, you won't know if the data is accurate or not. In the end, inaccuracy is the primary limitation of using self-monitored data. Still, self-monitoring can be useful because it has both informational and behavior change qualities.

In a study among bus drivers, we found that asking drivers to collect data on their own safe driving behaviors caused them to improve, even if they were not accurate in their data collection when compared to hidden experimental observers.[3] Researchers trained and asked staff in a residential setting to monitor their own on-task behavior and their compliance with planned activities.[4] Self-monitoring, paired with feedback and training, resulted in large increases in performance on schedule compliance and on-task behavior.

Self-monitoring has been used in many settings and targets in research studies for many years, including improving academic performance,[5] improving the performance of teachers,[6] improving the performance of athletes,[7] increasing interactions between staff and patients at an institution,[8] and helping individuals stop smoking and reduce their caloric intake.[9] There are many examples of the effects of self-monitoring on performance in the research literature.

We've seen many examples of effective self-monitoring in leadership projects over the years. One IT manager at an ABA agency wanted to improve project deliverability and timeliness for his team. IT staff are usually being pulled in many directions at once—people forget their password or have trouble logging into an important system, or they need other help that feels like an emergency—and this makes it hard for IT staff to work in a strategic way on things that are longer-term projects (upgrading operating systems, reducing cybersecurity vulnerability) because they are constantly being pulled away from these projects. So, the leader asked each team member to list the active projects they were working on and to log the amount of time they spent on each project daily. He did the same for the projects he was working on. They met as a team regularly and reviewed the time spent, progress, tactics on each project, and barriers they were experiencing. This allowed the leader to praise progress, help remove barriers, and coach or mentor his very inexperienced team multiple times a week. Performance dramatically improved.

A senior executive in a construction company was responsible for the company strategic plan and wanted to focus on that for her project. Yes, behavior change is not only for staff and supervisors! Over my thirty years working in organizations, I have only seen a few strategic plans work. I don't normally lead strategic planning initiatives, but I am often involved, so I get to see the process as it unfolds. Most strategic planning falls short in one or more of a few ways:

1. There is a lack of measurement and follow-up. People assume that, once you've created the plan, everyone will follow it. Not so, even if you involve them in creating the plan.

2. The elements of the plan are too vague, making measurement impossible, and fudging the numbers to make it appear that progress is being made is too easy.

3. The plan includes too much. Executing it becomes impossible and overwhelming to those tasked with implementing it.

The leader of this project tried to address each of these elements and used self-monitoring as well. Each element of the plan was broken into a series of measurable steps and managed as a project (and yes, this did involve a spreadsheet because of the number of tasks involved) and the leadership team members discussed the steps and divided them fairly across the team members.

The leader of the process then met weekly or bi-weekly with each team member (who monitored their own performance) to discuss progress on their assigned strategic plan elements and commit to completing the next steps before the following check-in meeting. The group came together monthly to discuss barriers or areas in which they needed input from the other group members. Progress on the plan was impressive, the team felt real momentum in executing it, and they saw the culture of the organization changing in positive ways before their eyes as the plan came together.

Self-monitoring also works for individual leaders who focus on their own behavior rather than pinpointing something for the teams to work on. Over the past five years or so I have seen a dramatic increase in the number of leaders who feel so busy with meetings and other required tasks that they don't "have time to think." Therefore, many leaders have focused projects on creating and protecting think time.

One leader found that she used to think during her commute to work, but now that she is working at home, she no longer thinks in the same way, so she planned it into her schedule and her measurement involved self-monitoring what she used the time for. She found that it was often interrupted, so she had to create new ways of maintaining the time without interruption. One way that worked well for her was to notify her team of her efforts to improve this and why she wanted to do it. Then she was able to ask them to look at her calendar before calling to see if "think time" was noted and to understand if she did not answer her phone or email during this time. Another client saw such success in his own think time that he implemented a weekly two-hour block in which no meetings were allowed, and the entire senior leadership team used the time for uninterrupted thinking.

In an example in the manufacturing industry, one large company was trying to reduce injuries on its sites so the senior leadership team all focused on creating and measuring thinking time in their calendar on a weekly basis to consider how their decisions were impacting safety on sites and what they could do about it. This was just one part of their solution, but they saw injuries reduced by more than 50% over a couple of years.

Email has also become a major point of frustration for many leaders. Some have reported keeping all email (10k messages or more) in their inbox for fear of needing a record of something and even using their inbox as a to-do list. Checking email in the middle of the night and first thing when they wake up is common among leaders, and both practices are damaging to your health or at least to your ability to think about your day in a strategic manner.

We have seen lots of projects involving email and all of these involve self-monitoring, including reducing email in your inbox, responding to all emails within forty-eight hours, setting clearer expectations about what the leader should be copied on and what they should not be copied on, reducing email checking outside of work, and checking email only during specified times of the day to reduce distractions and improve focus. All of these can be successful through self-monitoring the data daily and adding it to a graph and by some creativity in adding other consequences to change your behavior. We will discuss some of these later in the book.

Try it yourself

One exercise that we include in our leadership courses is to ask people to measure their own behavior. This exercise in self-monitoring teaches you what it feels like to have your behavior measured and gives you a chance to observe the impact of monitoring your own behavior in a systematic way.

The first step in this process is to think of a behavior of yours that you'd like to improve or change. To demonstrate that these techniques work at home as well as at work, I encourage people to pick personal behaviors, not necessarily something at work. Some examples of behavior that people select are:

- Time using my phone outside of work
- Time spent with family, partner, or kids
- Pages read
- Time spent scrolling on social media
- Minutes watching TV
- Time spent calling friends, mom, or grandmother

- Number of ounces of water I drank
- Exercise minutes or steps walked

The behaviors you could measure here are virtually limitless; just select something and commit to measuring it for two weeks.

Step two is to collect the data in a simple way. Usually this means making tally marks for when the behavior happens, but all the tips above in this chapter are relevant in this case as well.

Step three is to take the data, as you collect it each day, and add the data to a graph.

■ Times per week I call my mother

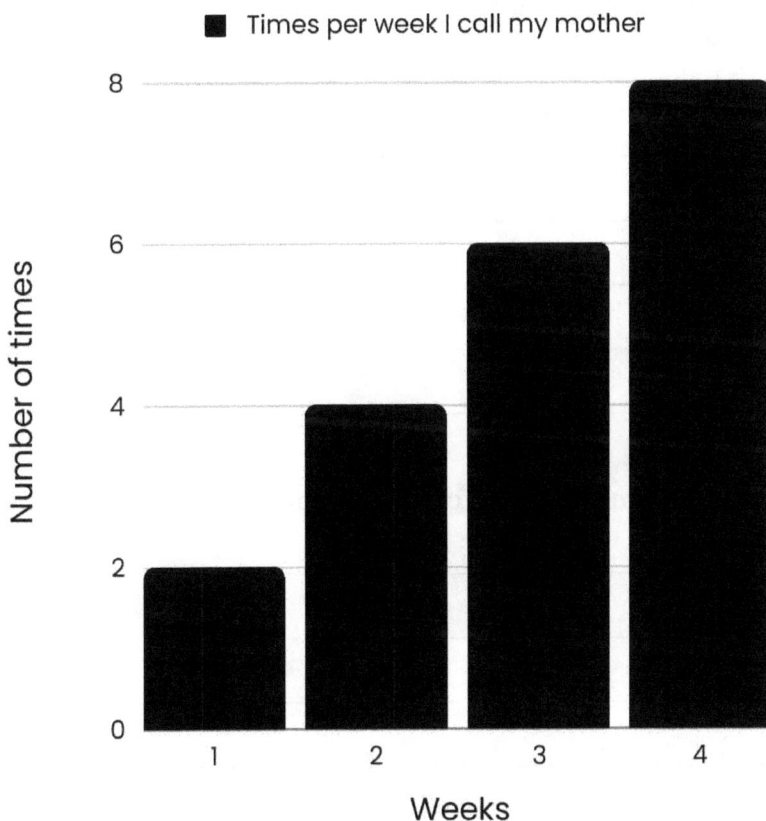

Step four is to reflect on the experience. Some possible questions you might consider include:

1. What did you measure?

_____

_____

_____

_____

_____

2. How much time did the measurement take? What would you change about how you measured the behavior?

_____

_____

_____

_____

3. Did your behavior change because of the monitoring?

_____

_____

_____

_____

4. If there was no change, what could you add to this situation to get a behavior change?

_____

_____

_____

_____

_____

5. What work-related things could you target using this approach?

_____

_____

_____

_____

_____

6. Could you see yourself asking coworkers to do this exercise with a focus on work behavior?

_____

_____

_____

_____

_____

In this chapter, we have focused on step two of the Behavior Change Process: measure. I shared some ideas and examples showing how you can collect data in a quick and simple way and use it to impact your behavior and the behavior of others. For people to engage in measurement, it has to be easy and satisfying to them. Making it satisfying might mean using the data to recognize them or celebrate, or it might be satisfying to them if they see that collecting data helps them do a better job. The worst way to implement these ideas is to make it threatening or to use the data against people. Always try to avoid situations that could make it unsafe to others to collect and share data on their performance.

Your Behavioral Leadership Project—Measure

Download a fillable PDF of this worksheet at
www.reachingresults.com/results-toolkit

Review:

What business result from chapter 1 will you focus on improving?

_____

_____

_____

_____

_____

Foundational pieces in place (mark "Y" for yes or "N" for no):

- ❑ Psychological safety: is it safe for coworkers to say what is on their mind?
- ❑ Communication: is communication lean and easy to understand?
- ❑ Behavioral integrity: do I do what I say I will do? Do coworkers?
- ❑ Self-management: do I manage my own behavior and keep my promises? Do my coworkers?

Step one: What is your pinpoint or target?

_____

_____

_____

Below, list the elements of your project:

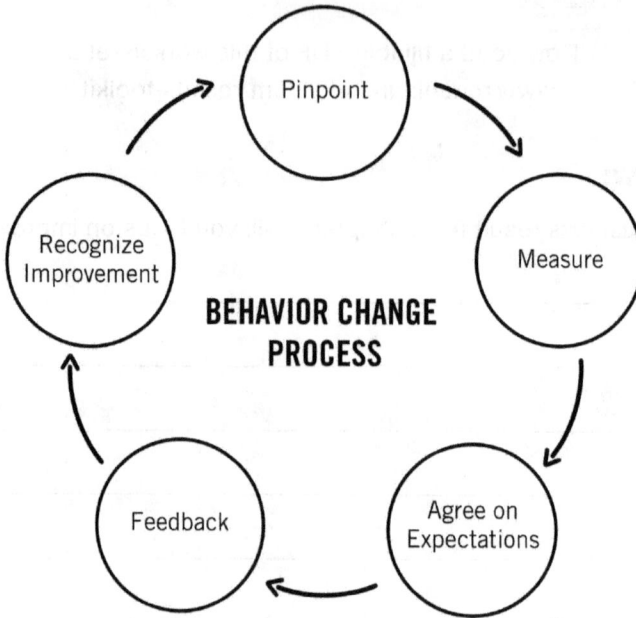

Step two: How will you measure it in a simple way?

_____

_____

_____

Now that you have a pinpoint and a way to measure it, go out and start collecting data on the pinpoint to get some baseline data. If this project is focused on your behavior, then take a moment to think right now about how many times you've engaged in the behavior over the past two weeks or so. Estimating is okay; you just want to get an idea of how often it has occurred so you can see a change when it happens.

As you collect your data, put it on a graph. You can use Excel or paper and pencil. Or crayon. It doesn't matter! Just create a visual for yourself.

Sketch out a rough draft below of what your graph will look like when it has data on it. Label each axis to make sure it makes sense to you.

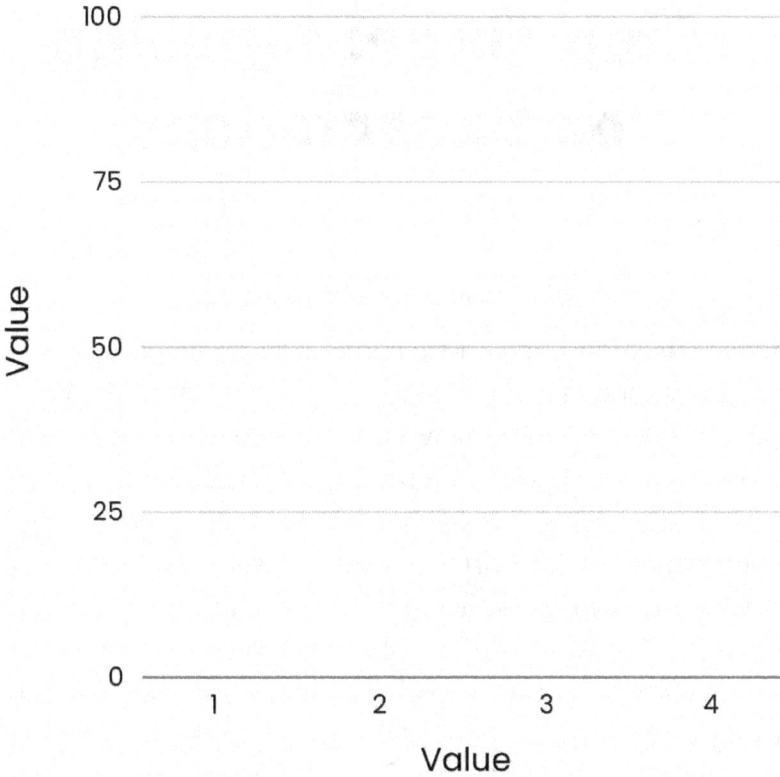

CHAPTER 5

Step Three: Agreeing on Expectations

The overactive imagination

I was coaching Lori, an executive who reported to Naim, a very entrepreneurially minded CEO. Naim was the kind of person who had more new ideas every day before nine a.m. than most people had in a month. Because they had a great relationship, Naim would share these innovations during his conversations with Lori. This was stressful for Lori because it was unclear if these were new expectations being added during every conversation. She tried to start some of these new projects up every week but just when she got something started, Naim would have a new idea and it was very distracting.

Vague "visionary thinking"

A variant on this theme is leaders who are "visionary" or divergent thinkers and who may have great ideas that they cannot articulate in detail—they can see the possibility, but they don't know how to execute on it. They hand these ideas off to their teams to execute, but the teams often fail because the expectations are unclear. Indeed, a vision is a few steps removed from an expectation!

It's kind of like hiring someone to remodel your kitchen and saying that you want it to look great, appear modern, and feel comfortable. Then you hire the contractor without any additional detail and they call when they're done. The outcome is unlikely to be what you expect because your expectations are too vague. We can all think of exceptions to this of course; if you hire an amazing contractor with an artistic flare then you might get a great product without expressing any clear expectations. If you do, you should hire them for the next job, too, though, because this is a difficult talent to find!

Changing expectations

Some leaders have a hard time deciding what they want to see, and so they change their minds frequently. This often causes confusion and frustration among their team. Kristin, a Chief Clinical Officer, wanted a particular executive to be "more decisive"—a label that is too vague to measure. Once we had defined "decisiveness," ironically, Kristin changed their mind several times over the following four months, saying the most important thing right now was to develop financial acumen, and then to make better business decisions, and then to coach their team more effectively, and then to improve quality, and finally to develop a strategy to fill seats in their new clinic.

I can understand why Kristin changed their focus so often—when business conditions change, we must react to them properly. However, it's easy to overload your team with too many new demands, getting in the way of their "real" work, and we must also account for the downtime and initial problem phase struggles that occur when shifting our focus.

Lack of engagement

Susan wanted her team to be more engaged. She told me how dissatisfied she was with their performance, and although everyone got along very well with each other and were collegial, there was a "spark" missing. When I asked what made her feel this way, she had a hard time explaining it to me. This can be difficult for leaders, but the first step in being clear about expectations with others is getting clear about what those expectations mean to you so that you can describe them using behaviors and examples.

In Susan's case, the examples she gave all sounded like "initiative." They included things like bringing ideas for solutions instead of just complaining, coaching your team without being asked, proactively reporting status of projects in an efficient way, and working with peers on new projects. Once these were identified, Susan could ask for, monitor, and recognize people for acting in these ways. When you begin to break things down behaviorally, it becomes evident that this is not rocket science.

It's not only executives and managers who have a hard time defining what they want and communicating it to their teams. A similar situation occurred with a frontline supervisor, Connie, who wanted her team "to stop coming to her with questions every five minutes." When we dug into the problem a little bit more and Connie got some education about pinpointing, she realized that what she really wanted was for her team to consult the manual to find the answers themselves before coming to her and asking the questions.

Connie realized that she was the cause of this frustration because she knew the answers so fluently that she always immediately responded when her team asked questions. It was far easier for them to ask Connie than it was to consult the manual. When she started asking if they looked it up in the manual and then paging through the manual with the team member to have them find the solution, they started looking it up themselves because that was much quicker!

Do any of these challenges sound familiar? I would love to hear your examples of failures in expectations and your solutions. We learn best from examples and nonexamples, and that's what these stories represent.

Many of the dissatisfactions I have seen among owners, executives, managers, supervisors, and their direct reports are directly related to one or both parties being unclear about the actions they should be engaging in. Let me be clear: I do not believe that simple awareness of the correct behaviors would instantly improve performance. This is evident in our everyday lives. For example, we know the speed limit and yet we exceed it. We know the recommended amount of steps, water, exercise, sleep, and diet, and yet we do not get them in all cases. The examples of awareness without behavior change are all around us every day. However, knowing exactly what to do and how to do it are essential elements to get a behavior started, and the science supports this assertion.

I have seen examples like the ones above in real life in human services, manufacturing, construction, retail, aviation, and other industries too. These are not limited by industry; they are natural things that happen when you get groups of humans together trying to accomplish things as a team. Knowing this inevitability can help us plan accordingly.

The importance and difficulty
of agreeing on expectations

In his book *Coaching for Improved Performance*, Ferdinand Fournies argues that most performance problems at work are far simpler than we think. Most are not the result of a lack of skill or lack of motivation. Instead, he argues that 60% of performance problems are due to unclear expectations. If leaders were just better at clearly articulating what they wanted from their teams, they would be far more likely to get it.

Russ Laraway mined hundreds of thousands of data points of leadership surveys during his time at Qualtrics, the business survey company, and found that one of the top three predictors of employee engagement is a favorable rating on this statement, "My supervisor sets explicit behavioral expectations."

Robert Schaffer published an article in *Harvard Business Review*[1] arguing that despite the hundreds of articles and books every year about new techniques leaders need to practice, one of the biggest weaknesses among leaders is simply setting clear and demanding expectations.

There are reasons leaders don't set clear and aggressive expectations, according to Schaffer (1991):

1. It may not be socially acceptable. If a leader suggests better results are possible, this can make their predecessor, their supervisor, and/or their coworkers look bad because they did not see the same possibility.

2. It increases the chances that you will see resistance from direct reports because demanding goals are, by definition, difficult, and if they are well defined then it will be obvious if they are not reached, making the team members look bad.

3. Leaders have the perception that if expectations are too demanding and people fail to meet these expectations, then there must be serious consequences. They would have to be reassigned or fired and perhaps the leader is reluctant to do this because they do not see this as the best outcome for the business.

Nearly twenty years later, Schaffer wrote another *HBR* article[2] arguing that failure to set clear expectations remains one of the top behavioral mistakes leaders continue to make.

I would add an important fourth reason: **leaders fail to pinpoint effectively and instead use vague language and labels** to ask for what they want. Often those labels are not even directed at an individual (i.e., they are often directed at a group or department), and so people aren't clear on how they can contribute to the outcome.

Earlier in this chapter I gave some examples of vague expectations like "a vision," "engagement," and "decisiveness." It is natural for you to have a vague expectation sometimes or to describe the result you want without pinpointing behaviors. In these cases, it's a great idea to coach the team and help them decide on the measurable, pinpointed behaviors that will produce the result. In some of my classes for leaders, we ask them to focus on ways they can improve safety (a label, too vague to be a pinpoint) and let them select the specific actions that would best serve their team and be most likely to work in their local environment. One person might select replacing tools on the tool board, another would focus on de-energizing equipment before working on it, and another might focus on asking about the impact of decisions on safety during planning meetings. The same strategy could work for improving quality, culture, billable hours, reliability, or profitability.

One benefit of studying Behavioral Science for Leaders is the emphasis we place on the practice of clearly defining behaviors (pinpointing). Over the years, I've been challenged in a number of environments (and in more than 10,000 improvement projects that I've coached) to help leaders to get better at setting behavioral expectations, and I've pulled in resources from various areas in psychology to arrive at a three-step process that works most of the time.

First, a change in mindset is required. My colleagues and I stopped calling it "setting" expectations some time ago and started calling it "agreeing on" expectations because the word "setting" implies it's one person's idea and you are being given your orders. We know that most people dislike being told what to do. We also know that most people are very good at "looking like" they are rowing the boat in the same direction when they are really not pulling at all.

In other words, you can create the conditions where people appear to be working toward a goal and saying all the right things at the right times but not really engaging themselves in achieving the goal after all. You can't tell what a person is thinking unless you make something come out of their mouth. Therefore, getting them to talk during this process is essential for you to know how they feel about the expectation and if they are likely to put any effort into this.

What you really want, especially when it comes to high level, demanding goals, is to have the person's full engagement, not simply their tacit approval to go along with whatever you have asked for. Your leaders are knowledge workers, not widget creators. Therefore, you want the very active and engaged brains of your coworkers and team engaging in solving the problems of how to achieve the needs of the organization. That is, you want them focused on how to have better ideas and how to execute them more consistently. This suggests that you should consider following a process that is more thoughtful than simply "telling people what to do." Instead, you want to create an environment in which they will be interested, challenged, and engaged. Giving them some choice and giving them a say in how they deliver the results produces more engagement. That's what this three-step process is about.

Three Steps: Agreeing to Expectations

You will want to call a face-to-face or live-video meeting to discuss the new (or resetting) expectations. This is not something to do over email because it is designed to be a dialogue. You should be able to do this in thirty minutes in most cases, but you might want to plan an hour just in case it runs long.

Prework

Come to the meeting ready to talk about your improvement project pinpoint—that is, the actions or behaviors and results you'd like to see from the person. To keep it simple and memorable, I recommend focusing this conversation on the pinpoint you've selected in the previous chapters. It is well-defined and you've already got some data on it, if you are following the steps laid out in this book so far. You can share this data in the meeting if the time feels right.

Step one: Explain why it is important

Explain the expectation or need you have and why you think it is important. Share the data you have collected so far. It might work something like this:

You: "It's really important that we all submit our completed session notes into the online system within twenty-four hours after the session. This is really important to the organization, because we can't initiate the payment process until the documentation is complete, but it's also important to client wellness because we can't make proper decisions if we don't have the completed case notes."

You: "I've been trying to figure out how to support the team in improving on this because I think it's really important to our mission, so I collected some data on it. The data tells us we are 56% complete within twenty-four hours." (Or you might learn something valuable if you can ask a question in a purely curious and nonjudgmental manner—"What do you think our team percentage is?"—and then tell them the correct answer.)

Step two: Ask them what they think

Ask them if they also think it is important and why. Can they think of other reasons why we should all be doing a great job on this behavior or things that you left out? You can ask now or build it into your coaching and dialogues moving forward, but it's also a good idea to ask them to think about what their plan will be to make this behavior or result more likely to occur.

After you get their input on whether they think it is important and why, this is a great time to ask them about barriers to doing this. In other words, what could get in the way of someone doing this behavior? Listen carefully and take notes. Try not to explain away their feedback—if you can get them to talk honestly about it, it's golden feedback, and remember that the learner is never wrong. If there is something you can do to remove the friction getting in the way of them doing this task and if you don't act on it, that's what we call *self-destructive behavior*. These elements make this process *a dialogue* and hopefully here is where you get some engagement and thinking from the person.

After this meeting is completed, and especially if they didn't give you much feedback about barriers, you might want to consider setting a new meeting with the team or various individuals to complete a Performance Diagnostic Checklist (PDC). As of this writing, the latest version of the PDC is pictured.[3] Others have created a PDC specifically for human services agencies, called the PDC-HS.[4] There is also the PDC for occupational safety (PDC-S),[5] and the PDC for parents (PDC-P).[6]

Performance Diagnostic Checklist

The Performance Diagnostic Checklist (PDC) is designed to help researchers and practitioners select interventions to address a specific performance issue. The checklist should be completed as a self-assessment or interview and supplemented by observations and data. When conducting an interview, we recommend interviewing more than one person, such as the supervisor and the performer or a high and low performer, to gather multiple perspectives. Once deficits are identified, we recommend rank-ordering deficiencies based on their likelihood to produce performance improvement. We suggest considering every deficiency an opportunity to improve performance rather than identifying the domain with the most deficiencies noted.

*This PDC is an updated version of the original PDC published by Austin (2000).

Describe the performance of concern: _____

_____

Antecedents and Information – This section is assessing whether instructions for the performance are clear for the performer.

Question	Yes	No
1. Is there a written job description describing expectations for the employee? Is it written in a way the performer can easily understand? (e.g., avoids colors difficult to see for color-blind individuals, in first language, avoids jargon)		
2. Has the employee received adequate instruction about what to do?		
3. Are employees aware of the mission of the department/organization? Can they tell it to you?		
4. Are there job aids in the employees' immediate environment? Are they visible during task completion? Are there reminders to prompt the task at the correct time/duration?		
5. Is the supervisor present during task completion?		
6. Are there goals set that are frequently updated, challenging and attainable? Do employees think those goals are fair?		

Equipment and Processes – This section is assessing whether the environment and processing support or hinder the performance.

Question	Yes	No
7. If equipment is required, is it reliable and in good working order? Is it ergonomically correct?		
8. Are there any personal barriers to using the equipment correctly? (e.g., fit, interferes with religious observances like headwear) *reverse score		
9. Are the equipment and environment optimally arranged in the physical sense? (e.g., tools stored near that area where they are used)		
10. Are processes suffering from incomplete tasks along the way (i.e., process disconnects)?		
11. Are these processes arranged logically, without unnecessary repetition? Are they maximally efficient?		
12. Are there any other obstacles that prevent the employee from completing the task? *reverse score		

Knowledge and Skills – This section assesses whether the performer has received adequate training and is skilled at the performance.

Question	Yes	No
13. Can the employee tell you what they are supposed to be doing and how to do it? Can they demonstrate it correctly?		
14. Have they mastered the task? If fluency is necessary? If so, are they fluent?		

Feedback and Consequences – This section assesses whether the consequences are sufficient to support and motivate the performer.

Question	Yes	No
15. Are there consequences delivered contingent on the task? Are they frequent enough? Are they immediate enough? Are they consistent/probable enough? Are they positive?		
16. Do the employees see the effects of their performance? (e.g., completed product)		
17. Does a supervisor or peer deliver feedback? How? (e.g., verbally, in private)		
18. Is there performance monitoring? Self/supervisor/peer/other (circle all that apply)		
19. Is the effort required to complete the response reasonable?		
20. Are there other tasks competing with the completion of this task? Reverse score List them below:		

Rank order the items you scored as problematic (scored "no" for all questions except those noted as *reverse score) from biggest issue to smallest issue. Choose the most problematic items to address the performance first.

1.

2.

3.

4.

5

6.

Gravina, N., Nastasi, J., & Austin, J. (2021). Assessment of employee performance. Journal of Organizational Behavior Management, 41(2), 124–149. Available at https://www.tandfonline.com

It may seem a lot to ask that you conduct a potentially time-consuming assessment of coworker behavior. In applied behavior analysis, we call this a functional assessment because it helps you to identify what is causing a behavior to occur. The causes are known as "the function" because every behavior serves some purpose for the person engaging in it. Basing your solution on the causes of the behavior has obvious benefits, but research shows that when it is based on the causes of behavior your solution will produce a larger and longer-lasting effect. In other words, if you find the causes and address them, you will solve the problem more quickly and with less effort, it will be less punishing for the workers, and it will last longer. That's why you'd want to use the PDC or one of its variants mentioned above.

Step three: Ask for a commitment and plan follow-up

Ask them if they can commit to working on this behavior that you've been discussing. If you have a part in it—either in supporting them or in practicing the behavior yourself, then tell them what you will commit to doing. Promise to share feedback over time to help support them, not to beat them up, but so you can both work on it to see it improve. You should demonstrate that this is not a one-way street, rather that you want everyone to be working on improving their own contributing practices. Research suggests that making a public commitment to engage in a new behavior increases compliance by a significant amount.[7]

Sometimes, though rarely, they will say they cannot commit to the behavior you've selected. In this rare case, I would suggest being very curious about why they feel they can't do this and circle back to the barriers and PDC discussion mentioned above so that you can understand why the person feels so strongly that they can't succeed. Your job is to help them believe they can succeed and to truly support them in getting the work done to a high standard. However, this doesn't mean that you do it yourself. You have a role and they have a role. Be careful not to accept any "monkeys" (the authors referred to *tasks* as *monkeys* in their landmark article[8]) that belong to someone else during this process. If this conversation turns difficult, emotional, or aggressive in any way, I suggest you take a break to calm down and come back to it later. If you need more resources to help you deal with difficult conversations about poor performance, I suggest Fournies's book *Coaching for Improved Work Performance* in which he outlines exactly the words you can use in these conversations.

Remember that you're trying to do the right thing in getting engagement during this conversation and trying not to push a one-way agenda. However, should the person refuse to do what is clearly a part of their job, you can always fall back on the fact that as a supervisor you have the formal authority to have a disciplinary conversation about their basic job requirements. If the conversation goes in this direction, please seek help from an HR professional to make sure it goes as smoothly as possible.

When should you use this three-step approach to expectations?

Sometimes you can simply tell your team what they need to be doing or tell them a result and ask for a plan to achieve it so you can coach to the plan. Other times, you need something more.

When should you consider using this three-step approach? When telling has not worked well or when you have tried other things but you haven't gotten the right results. Many leaders in my courses over the years who use this process and follow all of the steps have been shocked to see how quickly a behavior changes that they have been trying to improve for two years or more.

Here are some examples of situations in which I have seen this approach work well.

With an individual, team, department, or division you lead

Obviously, you can't use this approach with every expectation that comes with every job in the organization. However, for people *who report directly to you*, you can use this approach to agree on clear expectations on basic things such as:

- How to communicate with you (email, text, phone, etc.) and what to cc you on
- Expected response times for your requests or others in the organization
- How meetings should be conducted

You can also agree on more complex things in the job, such as improving quality of service delivery, increasing sales or profitability, improving billable hours, or other key results. In these cases and depending on the level of experience the person has, a great alternative to telling them how to do it is to ask them for a plan that you can discuss. The same goes for expectations with individuals on your team.

With a team of peers or coworkers you wish to influence or work with

In the corporate world, this process is often called "aligning" on expectations. It's a discussion among people who don't have formal reporting responsibilities to each other (i.e., no formal or hierarchical power) but who need to work together to achieve an outcome. Individuals are encouraged to dissent if they cannot "align" or commit to the expectations being discussed. Unfortunately, people often do not feel safe to speak up in such an environment, which is why this three-step approach can be very helpful among peers seeking to align on an approach to achieve a certain result.

For self-management

If your improvement project involves working on your own behavior, then parts of this process will be unhelpful. Here's how I suggest changing the process to better fit your needs when managing your own behavior:

1. **Reflect**

   Instead of having a discussion, reflect on why you think this change is important to you, your team, and the organization.

2. **Set a goal**

   Use this time as a chance to set a clear goal—how much are you engaging in the pinpoint now? How much would you like to be engaging in it?

3. **Remove barriers and add friction**

   Identify the things that make it harder for you to engage in the behavior and remove them. Make it harder to do the behavior you want to stop by adding friction or effort. Think of things that will make it easier for you to engage in the behavior and add those.

For example, if I want to eat less junk food, I remove it from my house or put it on a high shelf in my basement to make it harder to access. I might also add healthy foods that are ready to eat, tasty, and in plain view. If I want to check email only twice a day rather than constantly checking it throughout the day, I might close my email program, turn off notifications, and add an alarm or appointment in my calendar to remind myself.

In other words, you want to make it easy and satisfying for yourself to do the right thing and hard and frustrating or time-consuming for yourself to do the wrong thing.

Challenging questions and situations

Over the years, I have encountered some challenging questions from leaders who were trying their best to use and test these behavioral approaches. I have listed some of these below.

You want me to do this for everything I expect of my team? This is meant to be part of a process that you can use to improve performance in a specific area, so even though you should use it as part of your improvement project, it's not a blanket practice you use for everything. Not everything has to be a dialogue. Some things, such as coming to work on time, dressing professionally, and using professional non-aggressive language, are basic expectations and are clearly understood to be part of the job. Most people who have had other jobs will respect these practices, and those who are less experienced may need some special mentoring around these topics. Even still, explaining why starting work on time or completing case notes on time is helpful to many people and some data shows it works to increase compliance with procedures.

One reason you don't want to meet and discuss every expectation of the job is information overload. Additional information improves performance up to a certain point, but beyond that point the person can become overloaded with too much information, and this decreases performance.[9]

For this reason, and not only in the area of agreeing on expectations, leaders should reduce the amount and complexity of information that employees require. One way to measure complexity is through a grade-level analysis (free tools can be found online, and Microsoft Word has one built-in). Doing this gives you the grade level at which it's written and tells you what percentage of the population can understand it.

Isn't this micromanagement? No, this is called "management" or "supervision." *Micro*management is managing *more than is necessary.* If people are not performing the behaviors as needed, then they require some support from *managers and leaders.* It is remarkable to me how few leaders understand this and instead want people to "step up," "sink or swim," "show some initiative," and/or simply "work harder." These exhortations sound nice but are useless when it comes to managing behavior and more often will result in people leaving the organization rather than improving on their own. Agreeing on clear expectations is one way that managers and leaders can support their teams and help them to succeed. The rest of this book is about other ways in which leaders can support their teams.

Shouldn't executives or middle managers at this level already know the goals of the business? Perhaps they should, but more often than not, the reasons for disagreement on goals or strategy is that it has not been explicitly discussed and it has not been put in behavioral terms. Why not have that discussion and talk about actions, accountability, and timing for the avoidance of confusion or uncertainty? Uncertainty is stressful, leads to poor performance, and causes variability in performance. If you are deliberately allowing uncertainty to exist, that seems like self-destructive behavior to me. Uncertainty may give you more creative ideas from people because they don't know what the target is, but it also leads people to leave jobs for a place where expectations, outcomes and consequences are more predictable.

Who decides what is the "right" behavior? The "right" behavior is usually going to be determined by the work expectations that are set by department leaders, human resources, or operations in the organization. Of course, there are many gray areas that are not completely spelled out, and those cases can be managed by having strong relationships and conversations between leaders and their team members.

Azimuth vs. direction. I learned a great deal when General Jack Sheehan spoke at one of our conferences and he described strategic leadership as the military teaches and studies it.[10] Interestingly, according to their studies, one of the key components that military leaders get wrong is delivering orders (the military equivalent of agreeing on expectations). In their studies, they simulated a battle situation and asked people from top to bottom to give orders, and they recorded all the conversations. They were shocked to find that execution of orders failed in 60% of cases. Their analysis revealed that if leaders changed their orders from specific actions (Azimuth) to include *why they were asking for it*, execution dramatically improved, resulting in clear *direction*. So, instead of saying, "We need you to take that hill and hold it," leaders said, "We need you to take that hill and hold it so that we can accomplish X, Y, and Z." The proper frame for giving direction was then changed to, "We are doing X in order to achieve Y." Giving orders in this way allowed people on the ground to make better decisions and adjust based on what they were seeing happen in front of them, and this was a far more successful approach.

Why does this work?

In keeping with the theme of this book, it's important to understand why this works. There is some science behind each of the steps I have recommended in agreeing on expectations, and these are discussed below.

The ABCs

In the ABC model of behavior, agreeing on expectations is considered an *antecedent*. Antecedents are events that come before and prompt *behavior*, whereas *consequences* come after behavior and make the behavior more or less likely to occur in the future. It is said that antecedents are generally weaker than consequences, driving about 20% of behavior as compared to consequences, which drive about 80% of behavior.

One reason for this discrepancy between antecedents and consequences is that some antecedents are irrelevant to the receiver. We have evolved as humans to be finely tuned to operate on our environment so that we produce maximum reinforcement for minimum effort. Therefore, we are much more influenced by the *results* of actions. The antecedents mostly serve to tell us when something good (i.e., reinforcement) is available if we act a certain way or if something bad (i.e., punishment) can be avoided if we act a certain way.

The really useful part of this for leaders is to remember that your requests, meetings, policies, procedures, training, strategic plans, etc. (i.e., antecedents) will be more effective if they signal and lead to rapid and predictable reinforcers to people who follow and act on them.

Explaining why

People want to know why they are being asked to do certain things at work, and this applies to practices, procedures, changing tactics, and about any other pinpoint you might select as an improvement project. Studies have shown that explaining why it is important to follow a procedure can increase compliance with it by up to 75%.

Giving choice and input

Giving people a choice when possible is one no-cost way to improve engagement and discretionary effort. Research has shown that you can produce an 18% increase in discretionary effort simply by giving people a choice between similar actions.[11]

Asking questions

Studies have shown that asking effective and open-ended questions improves relationships, makes the question asker more likable, and makes the responder believe that you are more competent.

Public commitment

As mentioned above, we have known for years that making a public commitment to engage in a certain behavior improves the chances that you will follow through on your promise.

Using the knowledge that each of these techniques can promote success in its own way helps you improve the chances of success in your behavior change efforts. Try to find new ways to integrate these into your daily practices as a leader, and the science suggests that you will see a payoff.

Your Behavioral Leadership Project–
Agree on Expectations

Download a fillable PDF of this worksheet at
www.reachingresults.com/results-toolkit

Below, list the elements of your project:

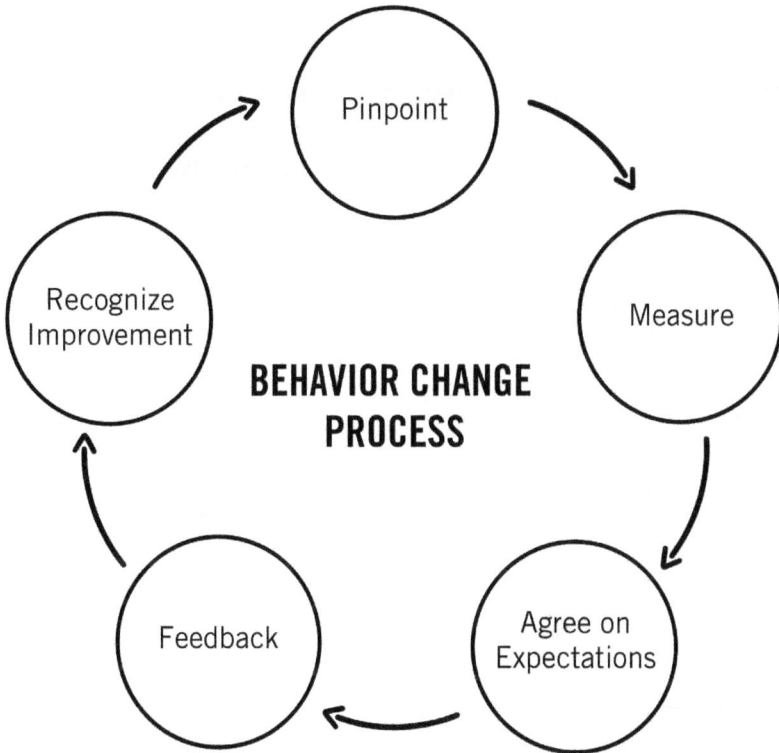

BEHAVIOR CHANGE PROCESS

(Circles: Pinpoint, Measure, Agree on Expectations, Feedback, Recognize Improvement)

Step one: What is your pinpoint or target?

_____

_____

_____

_____

Step two: How will you measure it in a simple way?

_____

_____

_____

_____

Step three: How will you agree on expectations?

Whom do you need to influence? (If it is yourself, skip to "Barriers.")

_____

_____

_____

How will you explain the importance of your pinpoint?

_____

_____

_____

_____

What did they think of the pinpoint?

_____

_____

_____

_____

What barriers exist to achieving the pinpoint?

_____

_____

_____

_____

Conduct a PDC or PDC-HS of the problem. What were the gaps you identified?

_____

_____

_____

_____

Continue collecting data on the pinpoint to get more data to share with those you want to influence or to see your progress over time.

Continue to add your data to a graph and draw it below.

CHAPTER 6

Step Four: Feedback

A commercial roofing company had a poor safety record and the owner was growing concerned that something more serious was going to happen. They had numerous minor burns and minor eye injuries and although the injuries mattered more to them, their insurance rates were also going up. Roofing is already one of the riskiest occupations, but this company worked on commercial roofs, which are usually much higher than even the largest houses. One of their competitors recently had an employee fall off the roof. Miraculously he lived, but he was seriously injured with a broken back.

When company leaders brought us in, we created a checklist based on OSHA regulations for their industry and collected some data for a couple of weeks. We collected data not through surveys but by directly watching the crews work. We, and they, needed to understand the current environment to inform where they were going. The crews welcomed us as we observed their behavior. They clearly believed (and told us how) they were being safe. The data from the checklists showed otherwise: At that time, their average safety score was about 50%!

We soon started giving them feedback on their safety behavior. We calculated a percent safe score after observing and then would leave the checklist in the foreman's car with positive comments on it every time they improved from the previous day. The foreman wasn't wild about this exercise at the start, fearing they would be punished for low scores and that it would get in the way of getting the job done. However, once he realized there were no negative consequences for documenting safety failures (in fact, there was praise for improvements), he became fully invested in the process. At the end of each day, he would come down to meet us at the truck to learn their safety score for the day. Then he would deliver the news to the crew. He even started bringing Gatorade and fruit to deliver if they reached their goal.

The crews improved dramatically after getting clear behavioral expectations, and consistent, direct feedback and recognition for improving. They welcomed the attention. These employees just wanted to do a good job, and their leaders provided them with specific, pinpointed feedback so they knew what to improve and how to do it. The percent safe score was based on the group performance, so no one was singled out or reprimanded. Rather than being defensive about errors, crew members were invested in improvement. Everyone involved reported that it was a positive experience for them.[1] The injuries decreased, leading to a massive reduction in insurance costs that year. The owner shared some of that savings with the crews as a bonus.

Not every feedback story has a happy ending, but it is possible to create a positive atmosphere where your feedback can be well-received, especially when people believe you are genuinely trying to help them.

Imagine you get a text from your boss that says, "I have some feedback for you. Come to my office so we can discuss." How does that make you feel? What is the first thing that goes through your head? Has this happened to you? Was the outcome positive or negative? When I ask this question during my presentations, there is often an audible gasp in the audience and even laughing at the question, as if it's obvious that they are going to be stressed in this situation.

No matter how you answered the questions above, we tend to expect something bad to happen when we're informed that we are about to "get feedback." Why is that? From a behavioral science perspective, it's because we have learned over time through experience and observation of others that "feedback" is usually negative, bad, or something that evokes an unpleasant emotional reaction. It's just a learning history that we're accessing here. There is nothing inherently negative or aversive about feedback.

Learning histories can be changed. Indeed, they do change, through experience and observation of others' experiences. What this means is that if you want a different culture in your organization—one in which people ask for feedback, deliver feedback to each other, and enjoy receiving it, then you can start today to build a new learning history by changing your practices.

You will need to start doing something different in order to make this happen and following the five-step improvement process in this book is a great way to start to make that change. In this chapter, I will first discuss how you can use feedback successfully in your improvement project. We get straight to what you need to know to successfully execute your project and deliver an improvement in your organization. Then we will discuss some tools and techniques you can use to make it more likely that your feedback will help you have better relationships, better conversations, and better performance.

Please keep in mind that everything about behavior change is context specific. For instance, some behaviors change quite easily after a single conversation, so you don't need to provide regular feedback. Other changes take months or even years and so require more vigilance. Pay attention to the situation and don't blindly apply the techniques. The best feedback a leader can get is feedback about the impact of their behavior on others around them.

> **The best feedback a leader can get is feedback about the impact of their behavior on others around them.**

Using feedback in your project

If you are reading this book in the intended sequence and working through your improvement project plan as you go, now is the time when you should start to give feedback. Before rushing out and delivering feedback to everyone, however, let's take a moment to create a plan. If you want to dive into the details on feedback effectiveness, I recommend that you read a recent review of feedback and its most effective characteristics.[2]

Here are some questions to consider when creating a feedback plan:

Who will receive the feedback?

Anyone whom you hope to influence should receive the feedback, but remember that you must have a relationship with the people receiving your feedback. The research shows that individual feedback is more effective than feedback provided to a group.[3] In addition, public feedback is more effective than private feedback. There are personal considerations in how you deliver the feedback, and you shouldn't do something that destroys the relationship in the name of your hopes for effectiveness.

If you do plan to present individualized performance

data in a public way, you should warn people about it well in advance. Ensure that they are prepared, and give them plenty of time to engage in the behavior before you share the feedback. Surprising people with individualized public feedback can backfire and create frustration and animosity toward the leader and toward other team members.

Who should deliver the feedback?

If you don't interact with them regularly or have a relationship with them, then their direct supervisor should deliver the feedback. The reason for this is that your direct supervisor is the strongest consequence provider in the organization. Some will disagree with me and argue that the CEO is the strongest consequence provider because they have the greatest amount of formal power. However, consider how much time a direct supervisor spends with their team and the strength of that relationship as compared to time and relationship with the CEO. You will see that the direct supervisor has the most influence over employees. Feedback delivered by a supervisor or manager produces the largest effects and if the supervisor adds their opinion to informational feedback it can double the impact.[4]

How often will you deliver updated feedback?

Most projects I have coached over the years plan to deliver feedback weekly or every other week. Behavioral theory would suggest that the more immediate and the more frequently it is delivered, the better the effects. The research confirms this approach, too, showing that weekly feedback combined with feedback after every observation produces the largest effects. In practical terms, you should consider delivering feedback frequently to keep people focused on the improvement.

How should you share the feedback?

Most people conducting projects want to share the feedback by email, but this can be a mistake. It makes perfect sense that your behavior of emailing sensitive information would be reinforced by the fact that it is much quicker and you avoid possible conflict or questions from the group. However, we also know that most people don't read emails (our informal data suggest 30% are "replied to" inside organizations), and when they do, 40% misunderstand the tone, and only 4% fully understand the average email.[5] I'm not aware of much research on this regarding feedback in particular, but we do know that face-to-face communication is thirteen times more likely to produce behavior change than electronic, written, or digital communication, and people are nearly twice as likely to follow a procedure if the supervisor has a personal conversation about it with the person.

On the other hand, my colleague Dr. Nicole Gravina reminded me that when people get positive feedback, some people will save it, print it out, and relive the experience years later. Of course, you can send praise in writing, but you might not want someone reliving constructive feedback regularly. However, I can think of times when being able to reread the corrective feedback was very helpful to me.

My advice is to be careful and let the relationship and context be your guide. Until you have evidence that it's safe to share electronically, share the feedback live and in-person or on video so that you can see their reaction.

On what should you give feedback?

For the purposes of your improvement project, you should share the data you have been collecting on the pinpoint you identified in the earlier chapters. If you have been following along with the process outlined in this book, during the expectations phase you already let people know that the feedback will be coming.

What medium should you use?

I have always been partial to graphs. They force you to get very specific about your feedback. Whether they are line graphs or bar charts, they should show changes over time. Ideally, they present the data so that when it goes up, that means performance is improving. However, I have learned over the years that many people don't understand how to read a graph. It's a good skill to have though, so you could teach them how to understand your graphs each time you present the data. For example, you can say, "The graph shows the number of times the behavior occurred on the vertical axis, and the horizontal axis shows days since the start of this quarter." The fact that many people don't understand graphs is probably why the research shows that using a combination of media (verbal, graphic, and written) produces the largest effects.

Your Feedback Worksheet

Download a fillable PDF of this worksheet at
www.reachingresults.com/results-toolkit

Complete this worksheet to develop the feedback plan for your
improvement project.

Who will receive the feedback?

_____

_____

_____

_____

Who will deliver the feedback?

_____

_____

_____

_____

Rate the relationship between the feedback giver and the feedback
receiver from 1 to 10 (1 = they hate each other; 5 = they don't
know each other; and 10 = strongest possible relationship). Given
this answer, how should the feedback be given? Does the feedback
giver need to do some groundwork to build the relationship?

_____

_____

_____

_____

How often will you deliver updated feedback?

_____

_____

_____

_____

How will you share the feedback?

_____

_____

_____

_____

On what will you give feedback?

_____

_____

_____

_____

What medium will you use?

_____

_____

_____

_____

Feedback Tools and Techniques

Feedback is interpersonal

The definition of feedback most often given is that *feedback is information that allows a person to change their behavior.* This implies that it's "just information," but it seems that feedback is almost always emotionally charged. Sometimes producing an emotional reaction is a good way to get someone's attention and drive them toward behavior change, but other times it overwhelms the person with negative upset, frustration, and anger. Personally, I've been literally driven to tears by harsh feedback in the past so I know how it feels. Some may argue that such an approach is sometimes necessary, but, fortunately, most of the time it is not.

This emotional reaction most often happens because feedback at work is *not* just information when it is delivered by people to other people. It carries the weight of judgment and other complex meanings that are hard to predict. Dr. Nicole Gravina created a simple way to characterize this fact by imaging two scenarios.

Scenario 1: You get feedback in a particular way from a person with whom you have an untrusting and uncomfortable relationship. The feedback produces a negative reaction and is received as mean, nitpicky, and condescending. It feels like the person is out to get you.

Scenario 2: You get feedback in the exact same way as presented in the first scenario, but this time it is from a person with whom you have a mutually respectful and trusting relationship. The exact same feedback in this case produces a positive reaction and is received as reinforcement, help, and support. It feels like the person is trying to help you succeed.

One takeaway point from this example is that in order for you to succeed in changing behavior, the receiver of your feedback has to believe that you are trying to help them. Take a moment right now and brainstorm a list of things you could do to make it more likely someone would believe you are trying to help them.

_____

_____

_____

_____

_____

_____

Your list is probably different from mine, and that's okay, because as we discussed earlier, this is all based on the relationship you've already got, the history between you and the other person, and the context in which you try any of these things. Some things I have seen work well include:

- Get to know the other person—their name, their partner or kids' names and interests, and any personal details that they feel comfortable sharing.

- Show concern for the person's well-being by asking how they are doing, reaching out to talk and support when they are struggling with something.

- Talk to them every day and be sure to talk about work.

- Tell them directly that you are trying to help them.

- Help them with things that don't give you an obvious and immediate payoff.

■ Give them lots of positive feedback as you see them doing good things.

Feedback is not always negative

We mostly think of negative feedback when this term comes up, but there's a positive side, too, and it's as important or even more important in the early stages of the relationship. Because of the often emotional reaction to delivering feedback poorly, and perhaps other more political reasons, too, most people operate in environments that are devoid of feedback until there is a major problem or until the supervisor is so dissatisfied that they are considering termination or transfer. I have heard people say that people tell a story about you at work and you're the only one who doesn't know it! This is unfortunate and unnecessary.

I've operated in highly political corporate environments where it is common for someone to share a thought or idea and then receive only silence in the room. It's fear-inducing until you get used to it. Either way, it is damaging and is a sure sign of an unsafe work environment. You would get much better results if people could even only say *what they liked* about the idea. Of course, the best results come from an environment where team members can share all of their thoughts and involve each other in a healthy exchange of ideas. These teams are rare in the business world, but if you've been a part of one, you know the power they hold. If you'd like to improve retention in your organization, creating high-performing teams such as these is an excellent way to do it.

People want your feedback

Leaders who are rated as better at giving corrective feedback also have employees who rank higher on measures of engagement.[6]

In other words, the better you are at giving feedback, the more engaged your team is. People report moderately enjoying hearing positive feedback, but they want to hear corrective feedback even more. Seventy-two percent of people said that receiving corrective feedback made a significant difference in their career. Of course, this all depends on how effective you think your manager is at delivering corrective feedback![7]

Despite our desire to receive it, we are often afraid to deliver corrective feedback, partly because we're unsure how the receiver will react and perhaps also because we're not confident we will deliver it well. If you want people to give you feedback, this is a good reason to always react well when you *receive* feedback, by the way. Interestingly, if people know they have to give corrective feedback to someone, their behavioral observations are less accurate. The assumption is that if they record only positive items in their observations, then they can avoid giving negative feedback. On the other hand, if they are not required to deliver the feedback to the person they observe, people record the data more accurately.[8]

You should go first

Even though it has not been closely studied in Applied Behavior Analysis, there is a preponderance of data to show that you will be more effective if you ask for feedback. Most of us would expect that *delivering feedback* would be in the top three leader behaviors when it comes to engaging people, but surprisingly it is not. Instead, "soliciting feedback" is more highly correlated with employee engagement, along with delivering specific praise and setting explicit expectations.[9]

Leaders who solicit feedback frequently are rated as more effective than leaders who don't. In a study reported in the *Harvard Business Review*, leaders who ranked in the tenth percentile on asking for feedback (they asked for feedback less frequently than 90% of their peers) ranked in the fifteenth percentile for overall leadership effectiveness, and those who ranked in the ninetieth percentile on asking for feedback ranked in the eighty-sixth percentile for overall leadership effectiveness.[10]

There are many reasons why people don't ask for feedback regularly. One of them is that we're worried about what others will think of our work and what they will say. Sometimes this is justified. I have seen situations in which asking for feedback goes horribly wrong because the feedback givers did not know how to skillfully deliver it. Some colleagues of mine called this "outlier feedback." It is purely aggressive, as if you've thrown a piece of meat to a pack of starving animals. This is not the norm, of course, and it can be fixed by publishing the results to the group and giving people examples of how to deliver corrective feedback more skillfully.

Ironically, we ask for more corrective feedback as we become more confident, but receiving corrective feedback is a great way to build self-confidence. You may be able to help people be more confident in asking for feedback if you first ask them what kind of feedback they would like.[11] For example, when getting feedback on their writing, would they like to focus on the content or the process or the message? There are other good reasons to ask for feedback as a matter of routine too. Asking for corrective feedback can help you learn what it feels like to receive it, get ideas on how to give it more effectively, and learn to perform better more quickly.

"Don't look back. You're not going that way!"

—Denis Morton, Peloton Instructor

Make it easy

Leaders are sometimes too busy to stop and ask for feedback. The remedy for this is to make it easy and lean. "Feedforward" is a process that takes ten to fifteen minutes and starts with the leader having an idea of something they would like to do better.[12] You can get ideas for this behavior by running a more traditional short anonymous survey of your team. We use an eight- to ten-question survey, containing various leader behaviors, such as delivers praise, sets clear expectations, and removes barriers, and some open-ended questions at the end.

Having your team complete something like this can give you an idea of some things they think you could improve. You thank them for the feedback, select one behavior, and tell them, "I'd like to work on listening." You have a series of one-to-one conversations with some of the team members and ask them their ideas to help you improve your listening, and you listen carefully to their ideas without commenting in any way. You say, "Thank you," and move to the next person. Leaders who follow this process and then follow up frequently with their team to ask if things are getting better or worse find that the team sees dramatic improvement in the target behavior. This works well because it is quick and simple and it gets everyone focused on future behavior instead of worrying about past mistakes.

Organizations love the idea of 360-degree feedback tools, and I can see why they are so alluring. In concept, you get feedback from people whom you report to, from your peers, and from your team, so you have a clear idea of how everyone thinks of your performance. In practice, they are too long, too vague and nonbehavioral, and often not truly anonymous (i.e., in smaller organizations it is often clear who delivers which piece of feedback). No one wants to spend

an hour completing an eighty-question survey, and therefore
the surveys are done too infrequently to help. Instead, you
should consider using something very short, behavioral, and
actionable. There are tools now that allow you to run "pulse
surveys" with one to three questions every couple of weeks
so that leaders can get frequent feedback and work teams
are not overburdened with long surveys.

There are many ways you can go about getting feedback
and different questions you can ask. Here are some that I've
seen:

- Ask the team to write down what is frustrating them
  right now and hand it in without their names.

- What is one thing you would change about the company if you were in charge for a day?

- What is one thing I am doing that helps you right now
  and one thing I am doing that gets in the way of your
  work?

- What is one thing I should stop doing, start doing, and
  continue doing?

You might not follow any of these processes or use these
questions exactly, but the key is to find a simple and quick
way to regularly get feedback so that you build it into your
routine and your team finds it rewarding to give thoughtful,
positive, and corrective feedback to you.

Make it anonymous and live

One of my favorite tools, anonymous live polling, is surprisingly rare to see in organizations. When using live polling,
you can build the question into a presentation (or you can
push the poll to people's phones even when they are not
all together), everyone responds at once, and then they see

the data in a nice chart. This gives the entire team or organization immediate feedback and it's normally very honest because people believe it is anonymous and safe to tell the truth. Polling questions and the audience responses can also be a great conversation starter for groups of people. You can have questions written by the audience, and these can also be anonymous.

In an ABA agency, an individual wrote a question asking who planned to be working for the organization in two years' time. Most of the leaders were taken off guard by the very low percentage of people who were planning to stay, and this kicked off a very useful discussion about the factors driving those decisions.

Make it safe

In a manufacturing organization, we collected over 44,000 data points on a wide variety of questions over a couple of years and these data painted a very clear picture of the organization culture. One person wrote a question asking if people followed a particular life-saving safety procedure when they were supposed to and only a small number of people reported following it. This caught the attention of leaders, who started asking the question more broadly, and they found that only 20% of people were following the procedure. As a result, direct supervisors started having small group sessions with teams, promising "immunity" (no discipline or negative consequences) for anything said in the meetings. The leaders learned that the procedure was too complex, most people did not understand it, and the essential tools were often missing, making it impossible to complete the task. However, this was not normally discussed because it was too psychologically unsafe for anyone to openly admit that they weren't following the procedure. Admitting you did not follow the procedure normally resulted in disciplinary action or termination.

You may not choose to use anonymous polling every day, and instead you might be *having conversations* with team members where you hope they will tell you the truth. So how do you make it safe for them to do so? The challenge for you is to figure out how you can make it rewarding for people on your team to give you critical feedback. I can't tell you how many times I have been talking to an employee at a client organization and they tell me all of the reasons a major, very costly initiative is probably going to fail. When I ask them what their supervisor said when they heard this feedback, I'm shocked at how few people have told anyone about it. The typical responses are "They stopped listening to me years ago," "I tried to tell them but no one cares," "They're too busy to listen to me," or they just laugh. The lesson here is to make it encouraging for people to give feedback and share their ideas because the recipients of your initiatives know the weak spots and gaps that can make or break your efforts.

How to receive feedback

I've said earlier that if you want more feedback from people, you have to make it rewarding for them to give it to you, and you have to react well to receiving it. However, what does this really mean in behavioral terms? Of course, there's a study on this topic.[13] Based on advice given by a variety of experts, the authors identified some key behaviors for properly receiving feedback and showed that these skills can be taught.

These behaviors included:

- Arrives prepared for the meeting—come with something to take notes with

- Maintains eye contact during the meeting—demonstrate you are listening

- Asks appropriate follow-up questions—show you are engaged

- Acknowledges corrective feedback—show you have heard the feedback

- Engages in active listening—show you are paying attention

- Commits to behavior change—show you want to change

- Indicates appreciation for the feedback—make it rewarding for them to give you corrective feedback

- Demonstrates appropriate overall demeanor—make it a pleasant experience for the feedback giver

You may not agree with some of these behaviors and may choose to change some or add others, but to me they appear directionally correct. Having a list of behaviors makes it possible to teach, observe, and give feedback on someone's ability to receive feedback. If you are trying to improve your ability to receive feedback, you could review these before a feedback session, you could ask your team how well you do each of these, or you could ask the feedback giver how you did on any of these dimensions in order to improve.

Receiving feedback that is very on target and about something important to you is sometimes very difficult and upsetting. In those times it might be helpful to keep a couple of things in mind: 1) painful but insightful feedback is going to have a bigger impact on you than innocuous feedback, and 2) imagine you are old and retired and thinking back at this moment . . . what would you say to yourself about it? In the second case, there is a good chance you might laugh at yourself for taking it too seriously. Most people in their old age and in their final days don't wish they spent more time at the office!

How to give feedback

Anyone who has managed or supervised others for any period of time has had to deliver feedback. I've had the good fortune to work with many experienced leaders, and in my courses I often ask them what they have found is most effective in giving feedback. Here are some of the things they tell me:

- Think about it first. Take some time to plan what you're going to say. When we rush into these conversations, we tend to do a poor job.

- Make it helpful. The best way to get someone to ask for more of your feedback is if you give them something that works. Something simple to change that produces a better outcome for them.

- Focus on the things the person did really well. We do need corrective feedback to improve. Focusing only on strengths is not as effective. However, most people are more likely to accept feedback if it feels generally positive.

- Related to making it positive, try to use a ratio of four to one, or more, positive statements to negative statements.

- Talk in behavioral terms. Be very specific about the behavior and the situation in which it occurs.

- Take a break if things get too emotional.

- Don't wait too long to give feedback. You will become too emotional or frustrated about it and then it will come out as too aggressive.

- Be ready to apologize and adjust your delivery if the person is too shocked or upset by your initial attempt.

- Ask a micro-question. For example, "I have a few ideas about how you/we could get better results. Can I share them with you?" This one comes from LeeAnn Renninger's TED Talk on giving feedback.[14]

- After delivering the feedback, ask the person what they think. Engage them in conversation.

- Have the conversation in a neutral location. Bringing the person to your office may make them uncomfortable. Going to their workspace instead, taking a walk, having coffee, or having lunch can be disarming and may remove some of the stress.

Get them to ask for your corrective feedback

One of the times in which I experienced the most growth was when I worked closely with Dr. Nicole Gravina. We had a practice of carefully observing each other and taking notes on the observations when we delivered presentations or workshops. During each break, we would eagerly seek the other one out to hear what was going well and what should be changed. Unlike most situations in which we tend to avoid corrective feedback, we couldn't wait for it! After it became second nature for us to do this, instead of delivering it all verbally, we would just find each other after the talk and hand a few sheets of paper with single-spaced observations on them. After everyone had left, I would find a quiet place and read all of the comments, using them to help me remember what I did well and what I could do better next time. Over time, we involved others in this same practice so that at one conference, I received pages of pinpointed and insightful feedback from six different people! Imagine how fast you can grow when you're getting that quality and frequency of feedback.

It didn't start that way though; we had to grow into that practice. We couldn't just decide to do this or be forced into it. We had to choose to do it because it worked and because it was so rewarding to help each other. We had to trust each other, we had to respect the other person's insights and believe they would make us better, and most importantly we had to believe that the other person had our best interests in mind—that the feedback was meant to help us.

One way we grew into giving this robust style of feedback was that we started by focusing on the positive. For example, I might speak for thirty minutes and she would have written down a full page of bullet-pointed behavioral feedback items; some of them were positive things I did and others were things I should change. But instead of starting with the negatives or "sandwiching" positives and negatives, she would only give me positive feedback. By the time she got to the ninth or tenth item, I would interrupt her and say, "Thank you, but can you tell me how I can make it better?!" And that's one way you can get someone to ask for your corrective feedback.

I followed a similar process in writing this book, wherein fifteen of my trusted peers and long-term clients read an early version of this book and gave me excellent feedback on it. A particularly transformational experience for me came from one CEO whom I have worked with for eight years. He did a close read of the book and spent ninety minutes of his time explaining his feedback. I was only partially joking when I told him it felt like a "tutorial on how CEOs read a book!" It was super educational and immensely gratifying to know that we trusted each other enough to have such a robust exchange of ideas. That kind of thing does not happen overnight.

Make it fun

It's easy to forget that feedback and growth can and should be fun. I sometimes study yoga, and my favorite teacher often says, "If you make a mistake, or fall down, laugh at yourself and get back up and try it again." If we took more of a playful view toward work and growth, we'd make progress more easily and we'd be more creative. One way I try to do this is by doing a short debrief after every event with anyone I am collaborating with. For example, after one of our conferences, all of the planners and speakers would get together and have a drink and some food, and each person would share what they thought the highlights and lowlights were. After co-delivering a workshop, even online, or after a client call with my team, I stay on with my co-presenter and we talk about what we liked about it. Invariably, we also discuss ways to improve, but we're having fun and a few laughs while we do it. *If you make it fun, you will plan in time to do it more often.*

What should I say?

There are entire books on this topic, so I will not go into great detail here. Some of my favorite books on this topic are *Radical Candor,*[15] *Crucial Conversations,*[16] and *Coaching for Improved Work Performance.*[17]

Instead of going into detail on what you can say, I'd like to share a mental model that I use in teaching feedback and coaching to leaders.

It is called the *response continuum.* The idea is that for any bit of feedback you'd like to give, there is a continuum of things you could say. For every statement you'd like to make, there is a vast array of different words and phrasings you could use. For example, imagine that your partner gets you a sweater that you don't like. What could you say?

When we run this exercise in courses, we hear a wide variety of statements that could, in theory, be said, from "It's not my favorite thing, sorry" to "I wouldn't wear this for a million dollars!" Some statements would work to deliver feedback and get the specific message across in a kind way, but others are too vague and not pinpointed enough to make the point. Still other statements are so mean, angry, or would produce such an emotional reaction that the person can't or won't listen carefully to your feedback. The goal is to find something that is both direct and kind to the person. Because you have a relationship with this person, you can say it in a way that you know will register as a reasonable thing for them. Don't fall for the "fool's choice" as described in *Crucial Conversations*. The fool's choice is the erroneous belief that you can be either kind or pinpointed in your feedback. In fact, you can (and should) be both.

When you see something, say something.

Hundreds of good things happen around you every week at work and at home, and yet we often focus on the few things that don't go as planned and get frustrated over them. Try this experiment for a few days or a week. Take a moment each day to reflect on what went well during the day. What good things did you see others do; what successes did they achieve? Now consider how many people in your organization or your family took notice of these things or said anything about them. In most of the organizations I work with, I see people give a carefully considered presentation and no one says anything afterward to the presenter. Someone runs a meeting that goes smoothly, allows for debate and engagement, starts and ends on time, and is fun and useful for attendees and yet no one mentions it to the meeting planner. A leader deals with an upset client, spends time listening to their concerns and makes the client feel better by the end of the conversation and no one notices. Someone skillfully asks for feedback or handles a difficult situation with grace during a team meeting, and everyone simply moves on to go about their day as if nothing happened. There are countless other examples, and perhaps I am just attuned to these sorts of "good" behaviors, but it is striking to me how often it happens and just how difficult it is for people to show their appreciation for the positive things that happen in their daily lives.

In response to this challenge, some have told me that it's not their job to help everyone else improve. In response, I say this: If that's how you want to live, it is your choice. On the other hand, you could find a way to change this in your own life and watch it spread to others around you. We all know that negative statements are contagious, but let's not forget that positive ones are also contagious.

Your Behavioral Leadership Project–Feedback

Download a fillable PDF of this worksheet at
www.reachingresults.com/results-toolkit

Below, list the elements of your project:

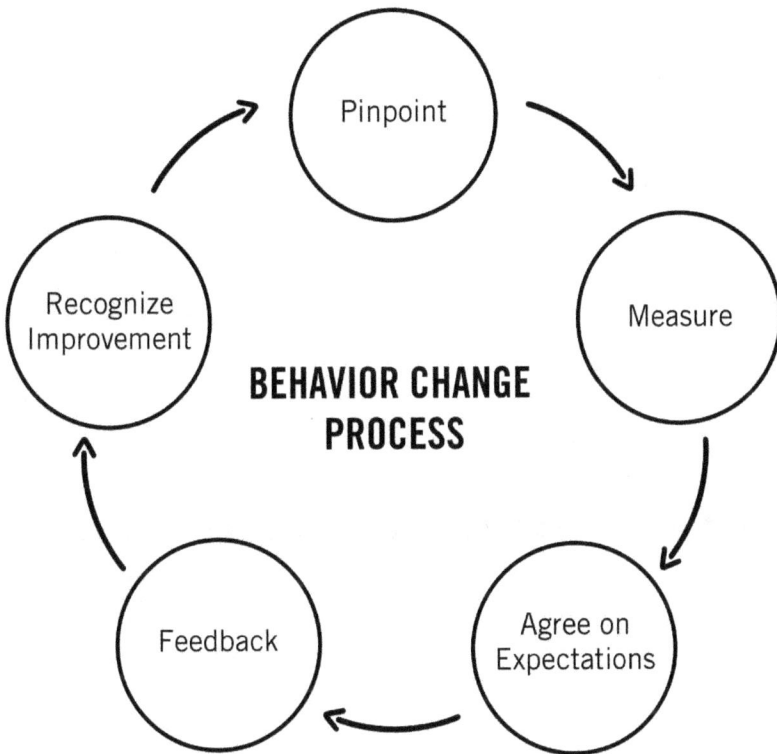

BEHAVIOR CHANGE PROCESS

- Pinpoint
- Measure
- Agree on Expectations
- Feedback
- Recognize Improvement

Step 1: What is your pinpoint or target?

_____

_____

_____

_____

Step 2: How will you measure it in a simple way?

_____

_____

_____

Step 3: How will you agree on expectations?

_____

_____

_____

_____

_____

_____

Step 4: Feedback. Describe your feedback plan below:

_____

_____

_____

_____

_____

_____

Continue collecting data on the pinpoint to get more data to share with those you want to influence or to see your progress over time. Continue to add your data to a graph.

CHAPTER 7

Step Five: Recognize Improvement

The Busy Manager and Reluctant Team

Laura felt completely disconnected from her team and wanted to reconnect with them. She cared about them and wanted to help them succeed, but they were all operating in a very high-pressure environment, and it felt like everyone had to stay too busy to justify their job. That didn't feel good to her, and she was sure it didn't feel good to them. Laura took my course and decided to focus her course project on spending time with her team. She started to visit their work area more frequently and she immediately noticed that when she arrived, people would suddenly disappear, run errands, or urgently have to visit other departments on campus.

To her shock and dismay, and through a few conversations with team members, Laura realized that the team was avoiding her. She reflected on why this might be the case and remembered how crazy busy this year had been. She realized that nearly every time she had visited the team over the past year, she had brought bad news, increased workload, or found errors for which she had to sit down and have difficult conversations with team members. Basically, she had become an antecedent for punishment!

To change this situation, Laura decided that she wanted to

become an antecedent for reinforcement. When she visited the department, she wanted people to come to her to talk, share ideas, and feel good about her being there. This wasn't an ego thing for her. She didn't mind being thought of as an enforcer of high standards, but it was clear that her relationships had suffered because of the types of consequences she was regularly delivering. This made it hard or impossible for her to reinforce good work when it happened. It was hard for her to use praise because she never saw the good things, and because people were avoiding her, she didn't regularly hear about them either.

Laura decided that her course project would be to deliver more positive reinforcement and specific recognition when good work happened. She met with her team to describe the situation as she saw it and worked out a plan with them in which she would ask the supervisors what was going well at the start of their regular calls and meetings. This helped her get a good idea of what people were doing right and then she tracked the number of times she delivered praise during the week. Instead of doing it verbally, she preferred to write a note by hand on company letterhead and deliver it to the person whose behavior she was praising. It may sound as though this is too simple to be effective, but the plan worked amazingly well. It was simple enough for her to carry out as part of her very demanding schedule, the team saw that she was paying attention to their hard work, their results improved, and they enjoyed having her visit the department because they knew something good would come of it.

> *"If you see someone without a smile,*
> *give them one of yours."*
>
> —Dolly Parton

What is recognition anyway?

In this chapter, we will discuss what effective recognition looks like and how to use it to improve performance. During this discussion, please keep in mind the pinpoint you are trying to influence in the improvement project plan you have been developing throughout the book and take notes on any ideas that occur to you regarding how you can use recognition in your project. The point of recognition is to create the conditions in which your target behavior becomes more likely. As you will learn, this is done through the process of reinforcement, which makes behavior more likely to occur again.

I will lay out some examples of effective recognition, explain some characteristics of it, and then provide a worksheet for you to plan the recognition for your project.

When I use the term recognition, leaders will often tell me that they "already do this." I am a lifelong learner, so I always ask for some examples that I can learn from. Listening to their responses has taught me a lot about what people think recognition is and what they think it is not. The most common example of the "recognition" that I hear from leaders is a program, such as Employee of the Month. I see the photo on the wall and special parking spaces meant for this month's winner at retail stores and office buildings, but also at manufacturing plants, hospitals, and service-oriented businesses. Even after all of these years of behavioral science research, this remains one of the most used programs for managers who seek an easy way to reward employees.

The problem is this sort of program is not recognition. Well, maybe it is *a form of recognition*, but it's not *effective recognition*. It doesn't reinforce any behaviors and probably does more harm than good. As I learned from Aubrey

Daniels many years ago, by creating a situation where one person "wins" every month, Employee of the Month programs are a great way of creating a bunch of people who feel like losers every month in your organization.

It's not only Employee of the Month programs that fall into this trap. I also see programs of awards given to employees at meetings for being top in the organization in safety, sales, quality, and the like. Many organizations employ written notes to recognize people who make big wins or accomplish difficult goals. These are somewhat better, but they are still too exclusive and they require too much effort to earn them. They would probably be fine if they existed in an ecosystem where lots of positive reinforcement and praise was delivered every day, but most of the time the general level of praise is low in these organizations and the programs were created to counteract this sad fact. They do not.

What is recognition?

Recognition should not be exclusive. We should work to democratize recognition. Everyone should have the chance to earn it every day. Here are some additional elements of effective recognition to help paint a clearer picture for you:[1]

- **Frequent and virtually limitless.** Why wait until the end of the quarter when you could reinforce behavior now and get improvements tomorrow?

- **Contingent on behavior.** This means that in order to earn it, you have to engage in some good behavior. Also, if you engage in the behavior, you should earn it regularly. It doesn't have to be Earth-shattering behavior. There are literally hundreds of behaviors every day on your team that could qualify.

- **Delivered consistently.** If the receiver is likely to earn the recognition after a specific behavior, it is more likely to have a positive impact.

- **Specific.** It should refer to an observable and measurable behavior, action, or pinpoint so the person knows why they earned it. It's harder to increase a behavior if the recognition is nonspecific.

- **Immediately follow the behavior.** The longer you wait to deliver the recognition, the less likely it will have an impact. Animal studies show that food rewards given greater than sixty seconds after the behavior have no impact on the behavior, whereas the same food given less than sixty seconds after the behavior increases the behavior. Humans are obviously different from animals because we have verbal abilities, but we do forget things. Waiting until the end of the year or quarter is a terrible way to remind someone of that valuable thing that they did months ago.

- **Personalized.** Personally hearing what you did well from a person whose opinion you respect makes the recognition more powerful.

- **Reinforcing.** It should produce an increase in behavior. If it does not do this or if people don't like it, then it's quite possible you need to adjust your approach.

- **Genuine.** I've seen leaders who walk around giving everyone a "thumbs up" as if this has some impact or serves as encouragement. Most people see such a gesture for what it is: lazy and insincere. If everyone gets the same thing as me, it feels fake.

- **Simple to deliver.** This is one reason why social recognition or praise is perhaps the best solution. This holds true as long as you've taken the time to develop strong relationships with your team.

- **Inexpensive.** This is another reason to use praise. Tangible rewards like a pizza party, coffee mugs, or T-shirts are okay to build some variety, I suppose, but they can also act as a crutch that managers use instead of doing the work to develop relationships that allow them to effectively deliver praise.

Intention vs. impact

When it comes to recognition and reinforcement, be careful what behavior you're reinforcing. The law of positive reinforcement tells us that you get more of the behavior you reinforce, even if it's not the one you intended to reinforce. When in doubt, observe and measure the behavior and let that be the guide of whether your program is working or not. Your intention has little to do with the behavior change; it's the impact that we're concerned about.

Imagine the person who wanted to get his partner a very nice, thoughtful, and useful gift to recognize their hard work. Now imagine the partner's reaction when they open the package and find a new vacuum cleaner! Do you think that would have the same impact as was intended?

A manager at a client wanted to motivate her staff to clean the facility at a higher quality, so she offered a raffle for her small team wherein every time they cleaned according to standards and passed her inspection, they got a chance to have lunch with her. The leader had a great pinpoint, they had a way to measure it, they agreed on expectations, and performance improved. However, when they started the raffle, performance declined! The leader discovered the hard truth that no one wanted to go to lunch with her. Her intention was good, but the impact of her recognition program was not what she had hoped.

I once visited a site that had a behavioral observation program that was employee-driven. They had a checklist and employees were supposed to conduct a few observations a week of peer behavior while their peers were working. They would then communicate the results of the observation to the person they observed. Sounds great, right? It would have been, if only the employees had conducted the observations. Leaders tried everything from requiring it to engaging employees in creating the checklist and system and training everyone thoroughly but nothing worked. In an act of desperation, they created a raffle contest, and for every observation conducted, the observer would get a chance to win the grand prize. The grand prize was a new pickup truck!

The program worked like a charm. It produced hundreds of thousands of completed behavioral observation forms across the campus. Leaders were thrilled when I visited to audit their program and provide recommendations for improvement. They were about to take a victory lap when they realized that employees were sitting at their desks and completing observation forms for hours each day, generating fictitious results. The leaders created a program that reinforced *completed data sheets*, so that is what they got . . . they did *not* get many more actual behavioral observations!

> "Don't count the days. Make the days count."
>
> —Muhammad Ali

The Individual Contributor

Gretchen was an individual contributor at a large public institution. Even though she didn't lead a team of people, she worked on lots of teams as a collaborator and sometimes as a trainer, so she wanted to learn behavioral techniques to work more effectively with the teams she was on. She noticed that the teams were highly negative, it seemed like most people did not enjoy their work, everyone felt over-worked and underpaid, and it was not safe for team mem-bers to share their ideas.

Gretchen decided that she wanted to work on delivering specific praise when she saw her coworkers do something good. She collected some baseline data and found that she rarely made positive recognition comments to her cowork-ers and she could not remember coworkers ever making a positive comment about her work . . . and, besides, wasn't that the manager's job after all? Therefore, her baseline was close to zero instances of praise, leaving nowhere to go but up, she thought!

Each day, she started the day with a reminder that she was going to be on the lookout for good things to praise and recognize. On day one, she woke up and saw one of her teen sons taking care of his dirty dishes in the kitchen. "That's strange," she thought. "He never does this!" So she thought for a second and then thanked him for doing this.

She always dreaded the drive to work because of the traffic and aggressive drivers. However, today she noticed that at one intersection, someone stopped to let her into the flow of traffic. She waved a "thank you" to the other driver, who smiled. She made it on time to her first meeting, and her teammate Heather gave a presentation that she clearly had put a lot of work into. It was thought-provoking, engag-ing, and challenged everyone on the team to improve in a kind way. Afterward, Gretchen found Heather and shared her observations. Gretchen was surprised to hear Heather say, "Thanks for the feedback. No one else even mentioned my presentation afterward, so I didn't have any idea how it landed."

Over the following weeks, as Gretchen got better and better at delivering specific praise for the good things happening around her, she explained to the leaders in our course how she started seeing positive things all around her. She was pretty sure that this was a result of her looking for the positive things and not some immediate impact of her using more praise. She explained how this was especially true at home, where she was seeing more good things that her husband and teenagers were doing every day. She felt like it improved her relationship with her husband and that one of her teenage boys even started talking to her more frequently. I think that was the most surprising result to her from the whole project! At work, team members started coming to her and sharing their observations and ideas that they weren't comfortable sharing with the larger team.

Using more positive reinforcement and specific praise for good work improves performance, but it also improves relationships and psychological safety. If you've ever worked with someone who is very good at delivering positive reinforcement, you'd know that they are someone whom people want to be around. Their attention is rewarding, and they make you feel comfortable telling them sensitive things that you might not feel safe to tell other people.

How not to do this

Delivering praise seems like an easy thing to do, but it's not. Sometimes our efforts fail, like they did for Sam. Sam worked with a really tough team of people and there was very low trust on the team. Team members did not like to talk, and they usually had some seriously negative body language on display during meetings (which they also strongly disliked).

Sam wanted to change the culture on the team and make it more fun and reinforcing to work together. He reasoned that if the team members used more positive reinforcement, it would change the tenor of the team. The team met every morning for a quick planning meeting, but typically only Sam did the talking. When he called on people to get them to participate, they did so reluctantly and said as few words as possible. Sam's idea was to encourage positive recognition during these morning meetings, which seemed like a good idea at the time. It was how he implemented the idea that made all the difference . . . in a bad way.

All the men on his team (and they were all men) were football fans, so on day one he came to the meeting and brought a football. He got eye rolls and sighs around the room when he explained that they would start the meeting with positive comments. He would make a positive comment about someone on the team, and then toss the ball to a person, who would make a positive comment about someone else on the team, throwing the ball to another person, who would do the same, and so on until the whole team had a chance to offer a comment. On the first day, 50% of the room decided to say "pass" when they received the ball. For the rest of week one, it got worse and worse.

Sam made a new rule for week two, where they couldn't "pass." They had to say something positive when it was their turn. The result was that the team delivered a series of backhanded compliments and straight-out insults during the meeting. The meeting felt worse than before he started the project. After a few weeks of this torturous approach, Sam decided to give up and he stopped bringing the football.

When Sam reflected on his project during class, he said it taught him a few lessons:

You can't *make* anyone do anything, really

We have the illusion that because we have formal power and a title as a manager in our organization, we can create rules that people will follow. In reality, formal power is the weakest form of influence, and in many cases there are people who will oppose

Praise is a discretionary behavior—you can't force people to do it.

virtually anything a leader tells them to do, even when it's a great idea. Just like disclosing personal details and saying what is on your mind, praise is a discretionary behavior—you can't force people to do it. You can't make them see the good things that others do, and you can't force them to build productive relationships with each other. You can encourage it, help them build or practice the skills needed, and create an environment in which it is more likely, but you cannot make them do it or make them change.

People don't like to be told what to do

Sam felt he might have gotten more traction on this project if he had started a conversation about it and asked people on the team how or if they'd like to do something different. Probably he would have engaged a small number of teammates, but at least that would have been engagement and not mutiny. Studies of high-performing teams show that the members ask questions more than they make statements. One target that some leaders have worked on in my courses is their question-to-statement ratio, trying to boost the number of questions they ask. High-performing teams have a 1.143-to-1 question-to-statement ratio.[2]

The effectiveness of praise depends on the relationship between the giver and the receiver

Praise is a social exchange between people. The words of praise only have real power if they are insightful and delivered by someone with whom you have a good relationship. Most people go through life at work not paying much attention to the good things that other people do, and even if they do, they avoid saying it out loud. For this reason, when someone shares a specific observation they have made about your behavior, it is sometimes shocking and remarkable to hear this thing about your behavior that you were not aware of.

Using Correction

So far our discussion of consequences has focused on using positive consequences to encourage more of the behavior you want. Most leaders and organizational systems underutilize these, especially given strong positive effects on behavior and outcomes. However, everyone is aware that there is a flip side to this coin and that sometimes we want certain behaviors to decrease. In this case you must use correction (also known in technical terms as *punishment*). Punishment or correction is a consequence that reduces the likelihood of any behavior it follows. No matter what the consequence looks like, if a consequence follows a behavior and that behavior is reduced, then you have delivered punishment. Correction (aka corrective feedback, or *constructive* feedback) is a more acceptable term than punishment and has less baggage, so that's what I will use here. Here are some additional considerations in using correction:

Frequency

As a practice, correction should be used sparingly and only for behaviors that are important for the person to stop engaging in. Aubrey Daniels taught me that the only reason to use correction or punishment is to increase the future chances of the person receiving reinforcement (i.e., something good). I think this is a great rule to follow.

Never correct out of anger or blame

Anger and blame turn the event personal when it should be about how to improve the outcomes and help the coworker. Even though we operate in a world where we are expected to assign blame when errors are made, neither anger nor blame helps you find a solution to the problem. A behavioral view of the world tells us that if someone is failing, the causes are in the environment that they are operating in and not something about them personally.

Immediately

Deliver correction as soon as possible after the behavior, for the same reasons as described above in using praise.

Pinpoint and describe the impact of the behavior

Kim Scott tells the story of receiving some direct feedback about her speaking skills when at Google. It was hard to hear, but it ultimately had a big impact on her career and required effort from her mentor. One day her mentor told Kim that saying "uhm" repeatedly in her presentation made her "sound stupid." Your correction might not be so harsh, but if it is direct (pinpointed) and helps the person see the impact of their behavior, it will likely be effective. I have seen many instances where corrective feedback was delivered and the receiver of the feedback was grateful to have it.

The sandwich

"Sandwiching" corrective feedback as the meat between two pieces of positive feedback (the bread) is a technique that many leaders swear by. However, experts recommend against this method for many reasons. The most important include that it reduces the impact of the correction but also reduces the impact of the praise that you added before and after. The process also can be seen as insincere, which can be damaging to the relationship and cause the person to assume you are not really trying to help them. Finally, it produces a unilateral event instead of a dialogue. Aubrey Daniels wrote, "sandwiching benefits the sandwicher more than the sandwichee" (p. 101).[3]

Discuss

Make room for discussion by asking the person what they think about it. This could be as simple as saying "What do you think?" and leaving some space for them to think about it.

Stay calm and nonjudgmental

No one likes to be yelled at, and it's hard enough to receive criticism properly without having to also deal with aggressive, emotional, or blaming behavior from your manager.

Focus on one thing

Try to find the one (or two) top things they could improve and limit your correction to that item. Most people can't work on changing more than a few things at a time. Keeping it simple improves your chances of success. I remember coaching fifteen ten-year-olds on my son's Little League baseball team. It seemed there were hundreds of things going wrong at any given moment. I could have tried to call them all out, but the more effective approach was to correct their behavior only on the most important items. Swinging bats in the dugouts was one of those behaviors, but so was keeping your eye on the ball when batting or fielding. When you correct more than one or two behaviors at a time, you may threaten the person's self-esteem, and this makes it hard for them to hear anything else.

When you find a vital behavior to correct and then reinforce, it brings with it lots of other good behaviors. In behavior analysis, this vital behavior is called a "pivotal behavior" or a "pivotal response."

> **When you correct more than one or two behaviors at a time, you may threaten the person's self-esteem, and this makes it hard for them to hear anything else.**

The Magic Ratio

After reading the sections above, you may be wondering how much praise you should be using and how much correction you are able to use without doing damage. Fortunately, there are data on this topic showing the optimal ratio of positive to negative statements in a few different environments. In educational settings, the most effective classroom teachers use a 5:1 ratio of positive to negative statements;[4] an observational study of high-performing work teams found they use a ratio of 5.6:1 and low-performing teams use a ratio of 3.63:1;[5] and happy marriage partners have been shown to deliver a 5:1 ratio of positive to negative statements whereas partners who engage in significantly more negative than positive conversations are more likely to get divorced. Researchers found that partners who maintain a high ratio of positive statements are able to repair the relationship when it is damaged.[6] This suggests that it takes five positive events to erase the impact of one negative event.

What does this mean for your leadership practices and your improvement project? It suggests that we often underuse and underestimate the profound impact of positive reinforcement on performance and relationships, and we often overuse punishment or correction and we fail to see the damaging impacts this can have on our results and relationships. Here is a challenge for you: What is your ratio at work? How about at home? Collect some data and find out.[7] It might be painful, but better to have a cruel truth than a delusional fiction!

Ways to reinforce behavior

There are innumerable ways you can reinforce behavior; however, you can try some of these techniques and observe the effects to get you started:

Here is a challenge for you: What is your ratio at work? How about at home? Collect some data and find out. It might be painful, but better to have a cruel truth than a delusional fiction!

- After spotting someone doing a thing that added value, required effort, or demonstrated their abilities, say, "Thank you for doing (name the behavior), you are very good at that!" or "I really appreciate it!"

- At the end of the week or month, get the team together and discuss what went well. Write it on a whiteboard and leave it until next time. One leader I worked with took pictures of that board, printed them out, and hung them around the room so you could see a year's worth of accomplishments in one glance.

- When someone does something well, ask them how they did it. People often like to talk about their accomplishments.

- Ask them for input on a particular challenge. If you use their input, they will want to see it succeed and be more likely to help out.

▪ Ask for a plan to solve the problem, give them praise and feedback on it, and ask them to implement it. They will work harder to make it succeed.

▪ Ask them to help a team member, and they will want to see the team member succeed.

Remember this is about making the person or team feel good about making small improvements every day. We know that small and consistent improvements will produce large gains over time. For example, if you and your team improve by just 1% each day, by the end of the year, you will be *thirty-seven times* better than you are now.[8]

Recognition Summary

I have purposely tried to keep this simple, to make it easier to read and easier to apply. If you are a leader or manager, you are probably mostly concerned with learning things quickly that will help you to deliver better results and to create a workplace your team members would never want to leave. In that case it is in your best interest to keep this all very simple and straightforward. In trying to do this, there are some more scientific things that have been intentionally left out of this chapter and others have been simplified. I will briefly discuss a few of them below, so you know you will need additional resources in these cases.

Recognition vs. reinforcement

Recognition, when used properly, can be a type of reinforcement. It's not the only type of reinforcement, there are many others. Many people misunderstand praise, recognition, and positive reinforcement. It's not just saying something positive, coddling, or being ridiculously nice to each other.

If not that, then what is the nature of reinforcement? It is when we operate on our environment and that produces an improvement in our situation. That improvement could be delivered by another person (like a manager or team member) or it could be naturally occurring (the task was fun or satisfying, we feel better, etc.). It works in both cases. However, it is helpful and motivating when managers can do things to make it more satisfying when people do good work.

Types of consequences

So far, I have only mentioned positive reinforcement and punishment, but there are four types of consequences that are each important. They are positive and negative reinforcement and positive and negative punishment. There is a time and place for every consequence type, just like the written word has a time and place for every letter in the alphabet.[9]

Schedules of reinforcement

The timing, frequency, duration, and magnitude of reinforcer delivery controls the type of impact that you will observe on behavior.[10]

Pay for performance

Leaders often ask me how to set up a pay-for-performance or incentive system to reward the right work behaviors more automatically. Clearly this is possible to do, but there are many ways it can go wrong. One of these problems is that paying someone for one result sometimes causes negative impacts on another important one. For example, paying people an incentive to bill more hours could cause them to be poor organizational citizens and refuse to help others out on things unrelated to billing hours.

In other cases, the pay does not impact performance because it is too far removed from the day-to-day actions. If you are moving ahead with pay for performance, be sure that you are rewarding behaviors or results that lead to revenue; otherwise, the system will not support itself. In the end, it should not be an either-or decision between using recognition or pay for performance. You will still need to practice effective praise and recognition to make your pay-for-performance system work properly. There are some books out there to help you go deeper on this topic too.[11]

Your Behavioral Leadership Project–
Recognize Improvement

Download a fillable PDF of this worksheet at
www.reachingresults.com/results-toolkit

Below, list the elements of your project:

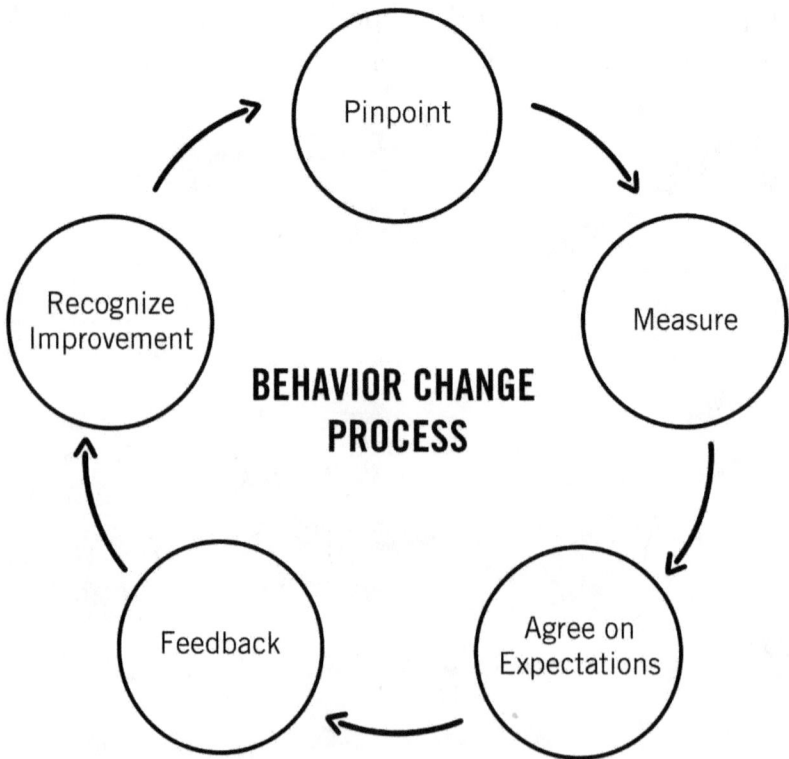

Pinpoint

Measure

Recognize
Improvement

**BEHAVIOR CHANGE
PROCESS**

Feedback

Agree on
Expectations

Step 1: What is your pinpoint or target?

_____

_____

_____

Step 2: How will you measure it in a simple way?

_____

_____

_____

_____

_____

Step 3: How will you agree on expectations?

_____

_____

_____

_____

_____

Step 4: Feedback. Describe your feedback plan below:

_____

_____

_____

_____

_____

Step 5: Recognition. Describe your recognition plan below:

What sort of recognition or reinforcement will you provide?

_____

_____

_____

How will you know when to provide it to them?

_____

_____

_____

How often will you provide it?

_____

_____

_____

Continue collecting data on the pinpoint to get more data to share with those you want to influence or to see your progress over time. Continue to add your data to a graph.

CHAPTER 8

Prepare the Soil

There is much we can learn as leaders from the practices of gardeners. Gardening does not start with putting seeds in the ground. It starts with creating a fertile place for the seeds to grow. This means selecting the proper location with the right amount of sunlight, clearing out rocks and debris, ensuring the soil is nutrient-rich, and aerating the soil to reduce compaction. Some of your seeds may grow without doing any of these things, but by doing them you can increase health and yield.

Applying the five-step process described in this book is like planting the seeds. Applying the steps is essential to creating change, but unless you have created fertile soil (i.e., the right environment), some of the seeds will not grow. When leaders say things like, "I tried behavioral techniques and they did not work," it usually means that they did not create the conditions where improvement efforts would work in the first place. There are some known practices that you can do to create these favorable conditions and dramatically improve the outcomes of your efforts.

For example, we know that developing rapport between managers and their teams improves discretionary effort. Discretionary effort is "going above and beyond" what is required at work or on a project. Developing rapport includes asking open-ended questions and developing relationships with your coworkers.[1] Open-ended questions have an unlimited number of response options. If you listen carefully to what people say in response to an open-ended question, you can learn a lot about them and their knowledge or feelings.

Creating a psychologically safe and inclusive environment is another great example of laying a solid foundation for change efforts,[2] plus people in psychologically safe work environments produce better results. This chapter teaches you how to use practices like these to create the conditions that can help to make your organization safer for people to succeed in applying the five-step Behavior Change Process and for people to engage in a culture of leadership development, behavior change, and performance improvement.

In this chapter I will cover the following topics:

- Create a psychologically safe workplace
- Recognize the importance of relationships
- Create strategies for building relationships
- Measure how your conversations are received
- Recognize that the whole person comes to work
- Learn, understand, and apply the ABC model of behavior

"Light tomorrow with today."

—Elizabeth Barrett Browning

Psychological Safety

People need physical safety, of course—and much of my work focuses on reducing workplace injuries—but people also need *psychological* safety. Psychological safety is the belief that the group you are a part of is safe for interpersonal risk-taking. In other words, if you feel psychologically safe, you're willing to say what is on your mind without fear of reprisal from individuals in the group.

Psychologically safe teams produce better results

Duhigg[3] described how Google conducted a study called "Project Aristotle" to examine what made their top teams better than their worst-performing teams. They assembled a team of psychologists to interview, observe, and test the highest- and lowest-performing teams at Google in search of the magic formula that would help the company create a better work environment for everyone.

We've all been on teams that felt great to work with and teams that felt stressful and fraught. Some just seem to work better than others. On some teams you can brainstorm with ease and come up with crazy ideas that might never work in a million years. But among those crazy ideas are lots of laughs and, more importantly, some bits of gold. In contrast, we've all been on teams that feel stressful and feel like we are being judged for our ideas. That has a restrictive effect on our creativity, and it's also less fun.

You might be thinking right now, "I'm not in a creative business." I'd argue that's not entirely true. Unless you are physically making a tangible product with the same recipe every time and have no need to improve or reduce cost, you are in the thought-creation business. That is, you and most everyone around you are knowledge workers. We know very clearly that knowledge workers need special conditions to think clearly, and this includes Google's main findings. You might be surprised to hear that my heavy industry and construction clients say they want a workforce that "thinks," too, rather than having people blindly follow orders without any situational awareness.

What Google found in their research project was that the top predictor of performance among teams like yours is psychological safety. That is group members feeling comfortable saying what's on their mind or sharing ideas with the group.

Isn't this obvious, you may be asking? Well perhaps, but despite its obvious nature, a survey found that 93% of workers are on at least one team where they do not feel psychologically safe.[4] Given these findings, the prudent leader would assume the conditions on their teams are NOT safe until they have clear evidence to the contrary.

Building a psychologically safe work environment is a big part of my courses for leaders, and there are entire books devoted to the topic. I suggest starting with *The Fearless Organization*[5] and *The Four Stages of Psychological Safety*,[6] and as with every book or resource I mention in this book, use your time wisely and start with a summary or TED Talk to get an overview before spending time wading through a thick book. The point is for you to use the techniques as quickly as possible. It's not to see how many books you can read!

How can leaders and team members create a safe environment? Unfortunately for many leaders, you cannot make psychological safety a condition of employment. It is mostly created and can be easily destroyed in subtle ways that are difficult to monitor and police in a compliance culture. It requires much more effort and consideration than in the old days, when managers had an "open door policy." That's far too passive to get the results you want and need, although I still hear leaders mistake this as an actual strategy. To make a change, you've got to do something that disrupts the current environment enough to be noticed.

Here are some ideas I've used and seen others use:

- Using surveys
- Conducting anonymous live polling as conversation starters in group meetings
- Asking open-ended questions
- Asking for input

- Recognizing someone's strengths
- Listening and paraphrasing what you hear to check for understanding
- Admitting you don't know the answer to something
- Showing some vulnerability, recognizing it when others do
- Using positive reinforcement
- Genuinely thanking people for telling you bad news or delivering criticism
- Normalizing failure

Reflection: Answering some of the questions below might help you to come up with your own ideas. Remember that behavior change is all about context, and yours is unique!

What activities do you currently engage in to create a safe space for people to have the courage to share their best ideas on your teams?

_____

_____

_____

_____

What would you like people in your organization to share more of? Perhaps you think of this answer team by team or department by department.

_____

_____

_____

What are the signs or signals that might tell you it is unsafe for people on your team or other teams? What would you see? What would you hear? What would you feel?

_____

_____

_____

_____

_____

What could you do more of to make it more likely that people will share their best ideas fearlessly?

_____

_____

_____

_____

_____

Pick one of these, circle it, and start tracking it for a short time. See how well you do. Maybe engage a coworker to pick one too and you can discuss how you're doing. Simply measuring it will probably help you improve. You can also use other ideas from the rest of this book to improve it.

Recognize the importance of relationships

I'm sure you are reading this book because you'd like to learn how to implement behavioral practices or you've got a specific problem or challenge you'd like some help solving. Perhaps you'd like to use some of these techniques that you've heard about or used before, like pinpointing, measurement, feedback, reinforcement, the Performance Diagnostic Checklist, incentives, or even pay for performance? It is important not to forget that all behavior change techniques (including everything in this book) are implemented by people for other people. Therefore, the strength of your relationships will partly determine the behavior change you get.

Everything we do is mediated by relationships between people. Relationships and history between people can complicate things and make it difficult or impossible to work together. However, relationships and history can also facilitate things and make working together a profound experience. We can do better work together. So, the first rule of Behavioral Science for Leaders is that *relationships matter.* This comes into play anytime we are trying to influence the behavior of others in any setting.

I used to think that mastering the techniques mattered most, and how my delivery "landed" with people was *their problem.* That's an old-school view these days and not in a good way. I think it's just not true anymore. Maybe it was never true. It was probably a symptom of my own novice approach and superficial understanding of what drives

It is important not to forget that *all behavior change techniques (including everything in this book) are implemented by people for other people.*

behavior. On the other hand, it's also not true to assume you can't be direct with people or use words to impact their behavior. So, in very non-behavioral terms, both are wrong: *being too harsh* without considering how people receive your

techniques as well as *being too hands-off* and assuming people will do what they will. If you *just hire the right people
and get out of their way then all will be well* leaves a lot to
chance. All will *not necessarily* be well!

An acceptability test

When considering whether some strategy or approach
would be effective at work, I learned a test from a colleague
some years ago.[7] He found it useful to consider whether
the technique you're trying at work would work at home.
For example, consider how your partner would react to you
issuing orders to complete the dishes by a certain time and
then you doing a direct observation of their dish washing
and giving them mostly corrective feedback. Maybe in your
house that would work, but in many households, that would
not fly very well and you might end up on the receiving end
of something bad if you tried any of that business. I have
checked with my spouse on the veracity of this claim, and
she agrees! So why do we assume that people at work will
accept the same techniques that wouldn't work at home in
a million years?

One reason I hear from leaders for not creating the right
environment is, "This is what we pay them for." That's a fair
point and a distinction from doing work around your house.
However, this point about pay is usually accompanied by
a discussion of why it feels like we must praise them for
every little thing they do (when we're *already* paying them
. . . isn't the pay enough?). The problem is, compensation is
the table stakes for participating. Your normal paycheck is
not an effective form of reward for good behavior. Most of
us get a paycheck for showing up at work, not for exceed-
ing expectations. You may raise the point about paying
bonuses for exceptional work, but in most cases, bonuses

are too disconnected from our actions to reinforce the vital behaviors.

The reasons for using praise are that it creates a more positive environment, improves relationships, improves performance by reinforcing specific behaviors, and produces engagement. If you have a free tool always with you that does all of that and then simply choose not to use it, I'd call that self-destructive behavior!

Hiring someone and then "getting out of their way" is often used to make the hands-off approach sound strategic and important. However, most people don't want to operate completely by themselves, and even if they say they do, this is not the way to bring out the best in most of us. For instance, we know that there is an *epidemic of ignoring* at work these days. Gallup reported that 25% of people feel ignored. People hate it *so much* that they would *rather be criticized than ignored.* Instead of talking to each other, leaders schedule their time to the maximum amount possible, with back-to-back meetings as if that means they are more productive, and then inadvertently ignore their teams of people who are doing the "real" work, assuming that training and pay will create the right environment for them to do a great job. Again, this looks like self-destructive behavior, and it is based on a faulty assumption that we can operate a high-performing organization based on rules, policies, and compensation rather than on relationships between people.

Strategies for Building Relationships

Create a relationship map or a phone tree

Improving (or developing) relationships requires that people talk to each other. The way this typically happens in organizations is through reporting structures. For example, you lead a team of people and you speak to them regularly. One problem with this is that increasingly we see that leaders are too busy to talk to their team members, so they find more efficient ways to do this, like email, IM, Slack, or text. These are all fine platforms for pushing simple information to people or getting information from people, but they are generally not relationship enhancing. They don't do a great job of gaining compliance with new procedures or practices either.

If you don't believe me, imagine only texting with your spouse or partner and never speaking to each other before deciding to get married. How long do you think that marriage would last? Or try the same thought experiment once you get married. Either way, your septic focus on efficiency would doom the relationship.

The way to develop and improve your relationships is by speaking to each other and spending some time together, either face to face or online (although the former is preferred). Interestingly, some research on communications suggests that relationships are built based on *frequency* of contacts more so than *duration* of contacts. So, you can do a lot on a half-day outing with your team, but if that's all you do in a quarter, it'd probably be better to divide that time up into daily or weekly bits and do it more regularly.

One human services agency I worked with was concerned about reducing turnover. They knew that a big predictor of turnover involved the strength of the relationships people had with their supervisor and other coworkers, so they developed a strategy to make sure that no one fell through the cracks in the reporting lines of the business.

The strategy involved creating a relationship map. During a meeting with all organizational leaders, they put every employee name on the white board (you may have to do this by department if your organization is too big), and every leader took a different colored Post-it Note and placed one by each person's name with whom they have a relationship and regular conversations. This gave them a strong visual image of the people in the organization who were being left out of the conversation, and they created a plan to address these individuals directly.

A slightly different, more top-down strategy was employed by another client I worked with in the construction industry. In this case, the senior leaders had gotten feedback that they were out of touch with what was happening in the field where the "real" work was being done. So, each member of the leadership team was assigned a list of people to call on the phone over a one- to two-month period. During the phone call, the leader would get to know the person a little bit, ask a specific question, and then take notes. For instance, they might ask, "What is one thing we could do to make this a better place to work?" or "What frustrates you?" or "If you could wave a magic wand and fix anything in our business, what would it be?" The leader who initiated the call would simply thank the person for their feedback, without explaining why things are as they are, and then they would transcribe the notes into a spreadsheet so that the other leaders on the team could see them. They spent time discussing it in their meetings. They fixed the things they could as quickly as they could. They reported back to the people who had the ideas on the status of the fixes and of those that could not be fixed or changed and why.

All of this had a profound impact on the culture. It helped people in the field to feel they had a voice, and it helped the leaders to experience the downstream impacts of their decisions. People in the field raised barriers and concerns, and the executives found resources for solutions to these challenges, thereby improving performance. This can also be a highly effective way to build relationships if it's done in a safe and nonthreatening way. You've often got to prove to people that they won't be punished for telling the truth but instead that it's better for them and for you if they bring their ideas forward and help in implementing them.

A manufacturing client's safety team was trying to influence the operations team to ask for help more often. The strategy the team employed was to divide up the names of all operations leaders and call them weekly to get to know them, discover any safety needs they had, and learn about their challenges. This developed the relationship very quickly and soon the safety team was in high demand. I have also seen this strategy work for other support functions that want engagement from operations, including HR, IT, and even accounting.

Learn about the person

This story was shared with me by my friend Jonathan Mueller at Ascend Behavior Partners and written up as a case study by Stanford Business School.[8] An ABA (Applied Behavior Analysis) agency was having trouble getting key individuals to accept job offers. The labor market was so tight that the best people were getting multiple job offers, and this organization wanted to be their employer of choice. So they looked closely at the environment they were creating during the interview process. They quickly realized that they were so busy delivering the work, they only spent a couple of hours with anyone who came for an interview. The interviewees would meet some members of the leadership team, maybe a few potential coworkers, and the HR director, see the office, and then get an offer or not. The organization would wait to receive their response, and it was "no" in 50% of the cases. The thing is, the leaders at this organization thought it was an extraordinary place to work and wanted applicants to see it that way too.

To make a change, first they extended the interview time from a couple of hours to one full day. This gave them more time to get to know each other. Next, they embraced techniques to help them understand each interviewee more personally and built it into their process. One example technique goes by the acronym FORD and it helps them understand what is important to people. The elements are "family," "occupation," "recreation," and "dreams." These categories, and others, formed the basis of some discussions with the interviewees, and it made it possible to do thoughtful things for the visitor. For example, on the morning of the full-day visit, the interviewee might arrive at the office to find a cup of their favorite caramel macchiato coffee with whipped cream waiting for them or some special gift from the company that was personally meaningful to the interviewee, rather than the typical coffee mug or water bottle that everyone gets. That personalization of the whole process made all the difference—they saw their acceptance rates nearly double to 90%.

Use reinforcer surveys

Many years ago, I was fortunate to have the chance to work for Aubrey Daniels, and I learned a great deal about performance management during that time. One of the many things that stuck with me was that when you started with the company, they asked you to complete a reinforcer survey, which they kept on file for others to access when they wanted to deliver a reinforcer for you or get to know you better.

There are many ways to structure such a survey, and you can find some examples in the book *Performance Management*,[9] which is a must-read if you want to learn more about solving performance problems and creating a positive work environment. When it comes to a reinforcer survey, the key is to keep it simple and short. Then you can ask to have it updated annually or semi-annually. However, don't just add the survey to your onboarding process without the proper intent. An approach such as this is made more effective and more powerful when your direct supervisor talks to you regularly and understands the context in which you made your responses on the survey.

Engage in planned conversations between supervisors and each person on their team

Many organizations have created complexities that get in the way of simple conversations that should be taking place daily. For example, matrix structures are increasingly common where you report to more than one person (and sometimes up to four people!), and I've found that these complexities often result in the employee not knowing who to go to. In addition, each "supervisor" is unclear what the other is expecting of the employee or how often the employee is getting face time, coaching, or mentorship. In human services agencies, this often takes the form of a clinical supervisor and a business management supervisor. In manufacturing or technology organizations, this takes the form of technical leaders and people leaders. Either way, it often causes confusion. Think of this situation from the employee's viewpoint. When you have a problem, would you rather go to the person you like and who will help you, or would you rather go to the person whom the written process says you should go to, even if they might not help, be accessible, or even care about you very much?

Data on retention strongly suggests the best predictor of whether a person stays or leaves for another organization is whether they believe their supervisor cares about them as a person. This is part of the reason relationships matter so much. How can you show that you care about your team members as people, while also maintaining a professional relationship, having high standards of excellence, leading the team, coaching them, and managing their work, unless you are speaking to them regularly?

In behavior analysis, we have a term for a single behavior that results in widespread positive changes in a number of other behaviors. It's called a **pivotal behavior.**

Some examples of pivotal behaviors for many humans include:

- Reading
- Communication or asking for what you want
- Empathy or taking the perspective of others
- Self-management and time-management
- And many others

For leaders, one pivotal behavior is having effective conversations. As noted above, we increasingly communicate via immediate methods such as IM, text, or email. However, 67% of executives and managers say productivity would increase if their superiors communicated face to face or by phone rather than email or chat.

The solution is to talk to your team, every day if possible. Unfortunately, I've found over the years that this is easier said than done for most leaders. There are myriad barriers that get in the way of effective communication. These include both supervisor and supervisee being too busy or too highly scheduled, poor relationships or aggressive behavior creating avoidance of conversations, or low emotional intelligence from the supervisor not "seeing the value" of talking with each other.

If you'd like to encourage this behavior in yourself and your fellow leaders, you can use an approach called "shaping." Shaping involves encouraging successively more complex behaviors toward an ultimate goal. We use a shaping model in one of my Breakthrough Supervisor Conversations courses to teach supervisors how to have more effective conversations using small steps. Each week or two, the supervisor will have a new focus, each slightly more difficult and time-consuming than the last:

Week 1: Don't change anything.

Pay attention to conversations you have. Collect some data on them. How many do you have? What is the content? How many people on your team do you talk with? Who gets the most face time? Who gets the least face time?

Shaping involves encouraging successively more complex behaviors toward an ultimate goal.

Week 2: Ask questions.

Think of some questions you could ask before talking to anyone. Ideally, write them down. If you can't think of any, Google it. Ask ChatGPT. Read an article on asking great questions. Whatever you do, just get some ideas to test. Asking questions not only teaches you quickly, it builds trust, and causes the receiver to like the question-asker more.

Week 3: Remove barriers and friction for your conversations.

There will be lots of reasons why you aren't having conversations. List them all out, everything you can think of, and start to remove those barriers and points of friction one by one.

Week 4: Learn some of your team's likes and dislikes.

What do they like to do? What are their reinforcers? Activities, foods, family, vacation spots, music, art, reading, TV, movies—the list goes on and on.

I have some people ask me if this approach is unprofessional or unethical for a supervisor to get to know their team. I feel that it's not only professional, but it's necessary for most of us who want to build relationships. Of course, if people don't want to share personal details, they should not be required. I saw one organization that took this too far and required people to share personal details that were designed to make them uncomfortable. That is not the purpose of this—the purpose is to deepen your relationship by **voluntarily sharing** some elements of your life.

One fun (and completely voluntary) exercise I use as an ice-breaker, thanks to Dr. Nicole Gravina, is thirty-six questions that lead to love. Based on a research study,[10] it's a series of thirty-six questions from least to most intimate. Of course, we don't try to get people to fall in love; that would obviously be inappropriate. We just want them to have a conversation and learn a little bit about each other, and these questions are a great way to do so. The study did not set out to create "love" either, but instead they tried to rapidly create a short-term relationship.

To keep it safe for everyone, I usually pair people up and give them an array of about ten questions and let them choose which ones they answer. No one has to answer anything that feels too personal. In the research study, the authors found that a couple of participants who spent time asking and answering these questions fell in love and got married, as did an *NYT* writer who experimented with the questions![11]

Week 5: Find out what they know and don't know.

At this point, as the relationships become stronger, you can ask more questions about work and continue to react well and stay positive when the person reveals something that could make them vulnerable. Admitting to things you don't know or are confused about is difficult to do for many people and requires a safe space.

Some questions you might ask at this point include:

- What is the hardest thing about your job?
- Explain how to do this task as if I were in my first day here and knew nothing.
- If I were new here, what's the first thing you'd warn me about to avoid my getting hurt?
- Tell me what you're doing right now. Why are you doing it that way?

Week 6: Ask what frustrates/challenges them.

Nearly everyone in any job has things they enjoy about it and things that frustrate them. Most of us are socialized not to talk about frustrations very much because we don't want to be seen as negative or complainers. However, you can unlock a lot of energy and underground knowledge by taking time once in a while (not every day or every week) to ask, "What frustrates you?" You will sometimes be surprised at their answers.

On a large, high-profile construction site, the most common response was "no toilet paper in the bathrooms." This was much to the disappointment of the leaders, who were hoping for "more robust feedback" or something more exciting. In an ABA agency that had a major IT project going on where contractors were behind schedule, the organization leaders found that many contractors did not have the sign-in credentials required to do the work. "Why didn't they just tell us?" could be heard in the hallways. In another agency, the leaders all complained about being constantly interrupted and never having time to think, not even during my course. This caused me to ask two more questions and I found that they all had push notifications on for Teams and for their email, so they were seeing a snippet of *every email* that arrived during my class. After they learned to turn these notifications off, they were much happier. And so was I.

Try this and I think you may be surprised.

Week 7: Mention positive things they are doing.

Go and see someone doing the work, observe them for a few minutes and find something genuine, specific, and positive to say to them about their work. It must be thoughtful and refer to something specific that takes some effort on their part or else it could be seen as insulting or condescending. The person must believe that you have their best interests at heart in order for this to land well for them.

One time I was teaching frontline supervisors to use these techniques and one of them tried it. He said he went to a person who had thirty-five years on the manufacturing floor and said, "I like the way you lifted that metal." The worker turned to him and said, "F*** you!" and walked away.

Clearly, a response like this is wildly inappropriate and could get you immediately fired in many organizations. On the other hand, perhaps this supervisor did not have the relationship built to give him the privilege of delivering reinforcement to that person.

Reflection

Take some time to think of each person on your team, and for each of them, consider what they do well. List it below, and then make it a point to go and tell them. That's a great way to kick this off. If you can't think of anything, then you've got to learn more about that team member and give it some more thought.

_____

_____

_____

_____

_____

Measure How Your Conversations Are Received

We've found the message that managers believe they are sending is not always the message that their team is hearing. It is important to note that communication is measured at the receiver's ear, not at the speaker's lips.[12]

So how do we use this knowledge? In one company, we wondered what kinds of safety-related conversations people were having with their supervisors. To find out, we asked their supervisors to report the content and frequency of their conversations, and then we asked people who worked for these same supervisors to report the last thing they talked about with their supervisor.

The results were surprising to everyone. They did not usually agree with each other regarding what they talked about. However, giving supervisors feedback on what their teams had heard helped the supervisors to improve. This site had its best year on record for safety after starting this process of communication measurement.

In the figures seen here, each bar represents a week's

Reported Conversations vs. Received Conversations

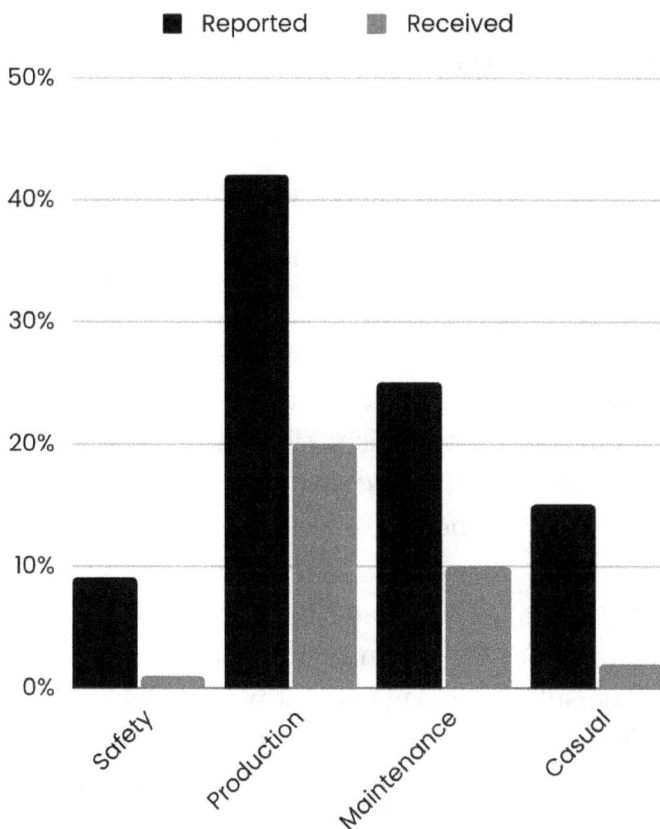

■ Reported   ▨ Received

50%

40%

30%

20%

10%

0%

Safety   Production   Maintenance   Casual

worth of data. On the left are the reports from supervisors
on what they discussed. On the right are the reports from
the workers on what they remember hearing. As you can see,
the supervisors' reports did not always match the workers'
memories. In this case, we wanted supervisors to talk about
safety more frequently and in more memorable ways, and
they eventually got there, but it required them to focus on
safety during at least 50% of their conversations!

What do you want your supervisors or coworkers talking
about? How much do you hope they are learning about

their teams' experiences? How quickly do you think they can respond if one of their team members is struggling? Do they even know about the struggles, or is that conversation left for the exit interview?

The whole person comes to work

"One cannot hire a hand; the whole [person] always comes with it."

—Peter Drucker

When creating the conditions for our behavioral techniques to work, we sometimes forget that we're dealing with other humans. I know this topic is very related to the preceding items; however, I think it deserves a special place of its own. More and more we hear leaders say, "The whole person comes to work."

Of course the whole person comes to work, in a literal sense. But the saying means more than meets the eye, I believe. The subtle message is that we assume we can rent a person's behavior (as I've seen many management writers claim) without getting the "other stuff" that comes with it. It's so common these days that a TV series (*Severance*) portrayed a company that placed a chip in employees' brains (who volunteered for the procedure) to help them "sever" their work life from their personal life. This concept truly is science fiction and calls into question whether work–life balance is ever even possible. Combine this with the remote work movement that many of us were forced into during the height of the COVID pandemic, and we see how work has crept into all aspects of our lives. The line between working and "not working" has become blurred for many of us.

Bring this concept into the workplace and what you have is the idea that people should be treated like the fallible humans we are. We make mistakes. We sometimes don't feel well or get enough rest or forget things or don't plan well enough or work too many hours, and this affects how we perform at work and in life. It is also acknowledgment that mental health plays an enormous role in our well-being, physical health, happiness, and work.

Someone who has cancer or mental illness or addiction or is hungry has that condition at work *and* at home. That's not just true for medical or psychological conditions but also for practices, education, and life skills. *Maverick* author Ricardo Semler[13] completely democratized his business (including allowing teams, not leaders alone, to choose to hire new members or not) and while doing so taught employees how to read the company's financial reports, how to balance their checkbooks, how to eat a healthy diet and cook, and other life skills. When he had to lay people off during economic downturns, he helped them start their own businesses and gave them low-interest loans or machinery leases. Needless to say, the line of people wanting to work for him was quite long.

Does your organization recognize that the whole person comes to work? How do people feel they need to act to "fit into" your culture? How many potentially great people do those norms alienate?

I am not suggesting you should not have norms of pro-fessionalism, accountability, and effectiveness. Rather, I am suggesting that we all deserve some grace and should give some to others too. More than that—giving people the safety they need to fully contribute at work allows them to develop into their best selves, which is great for them and for you.

There are many activities that go into creating strong relationships at work. However, being able to effectively develop relationships is a competitive advantage. The reason it gives you an advantage is that it helps your leaders to create the right environment to deliver the behaviors and results important to your organization. You will be able to deliver all of these techniques better if you educate your leaders in behavioral science more deeply too. The next section explains one way to do that.

Learn, Understand, and Apply the ABC Model of Behavior

One way we can deepen our understanding of the environment and its impact on behavior is through learning the ABC model of behavior. The ABC model is the set of organizing principles behind most behavioral science techniques. At a high level, the ABC model of behavior tells us that behavior occurs because of events that come before it (antecedents) and events that come after it (consequences). The antecedents and the consequences are the specific elements involved in "creating the right environment" as we have used that phrase throughout this book.

Antecedents in organizations might include training, meetings, emails, the physical environment, prompts, reminders, and other things. Antecedents are anything that might occasion (or some would say "trigger") a behavior.

Once the behavior occurs, the events that happen afterward are considered consequences. These are pleasant or unpleasant to the receiver. We are not only talking about "bad" or "negative" consequences here. Many leaders whom I teach naturally assume that the word "consequences" means something bad.

In fact, as we have discussed in earlier chapters, positive consequences are preferable to negative (also known as "aversive") consequences, for a variety of reasons. Some examples of consequences include a smile, praise, critical feedback, or incentives. The strongest consequences occur immediately after the behavior and occur reliably (e.g., the immediate and reliable consequence to turning the key to your car is that your car starts). The weakest consequences are very delayed and appear unlikely to the performer (e.g., getting sick from smoking).

Once you have a fluent understanding of this model, knowing antecedents, consequences, and what makes some consequences stronger than others can be very useful for you in creating the right environment for people at work. It is also useful for parents at home or for anyone influencing the behavior of themselves or others in any setting. In my experience, this is not just useful for leaders to understand, but leaders can effectively use the ABC analysis as a tool to start discussions with the workforce about the drivers of their own behavior, helping them to feel more control over their environment but also helping the leaders to learn about what is influencing key behaviors and results.

I saw this happen on a large construction site. They had the problem of tradespeople not cleaning up material scraps and trash after themselves (this is called "housekeeping" in the construction world, and when it is poorly done it drives a high percentage of injuries). After the superintendent learned about the ABC model, he brought the foremen and their teams together in a big room and pulled up a whiteboard with markers. He pinpointed the problem: "Doing work without cleaning up after yourself" and without using the word "antecedent," he asked them, "What happens before the job that gets in the way of cleaning up?" "When you walk onto the site, what conditions might cause you to clean up or not clean up?" Then he got them thinking about consequences, without naming the word, by asking them, "What do you get out of moving to the next room or leaving the site without cleaning up?" "After you've created a mess, what gets in the way of cleaning it up?" "Does your foreman ever talk to you about cleaning up?" They generated a list of things that were drivers of this key behavior on their site, and it gave them ideas for how to address the problem. They added garbage containers and they started to take and submit an area housekeeping photo before moving to the next area. Their foreman committed to commenting on the photos, walking through the areas to check the team's work, and praising people for good housekeeping.

One thing that gets in the way of leaders using this ABC model effectively is that antecedents and consequences are not equally effective. Specifically, many have argued that there is an 80/20 relationship between them. In this case, antecedents are said to drive 20% of behavior and consequences are said to drive 80% of behavior. In other words, antecedents tend to be a weaker behavior change tool than consequences. Consider the example of a speed sign (antecedent) that has no impact on our driving speed. Which of these is more likely to impact your speed: a speed sign (antecedent) or a police car (antecedent that signals a potential consequence)? Weak antecedents similar to the speed sign are a cause of many of the poor practices that plague leaders and managers. If you are at a workplace office, you probably have a bunch of weak antecedents around you right now.

Add to this the fact that it is generally easier to write a procedure or issue a new policy (antecedents) than it is to monitor and give feedback and praise on whether or not the procedure is being followed (consequences). The result is that you have legions of leaders around the world who try to lead with antecedents rather than consequences. Or, in other words, *they lead with one arm tied behind their back!*

There is evidence to support my claims. If you look at the

research, you will find that clarifying the behaviors expected of someone at work results in a 10–15% increase in those behaviors.[14] On the other hand, when you add feedback and praise for those same behaviors, you tend to see a 50–100% increase. This effect has been demonstrated hundreds of times since the 1970s; it is very reliable.

If you are at a workplace office, you probably have a bunch of weak antecedents around you right now.

How can you use this information about the ABCs? You wouldn't want to apply this to every behavior in your organization. It would be impossible and make you too busy. You've got to get very good at helping your teams to find vital behaviors to which this thinking can be applied. This behavioral approach is highly effective, but it takes time and effort, and in organizations, behavior costs money. The goal in organizations is to improve results *efficiently*. If you can produce the same result in less time and less effort, then it is more valuable. Choose your pinpoints wisely and keep practicing the ABC model.

What this might look like . . .

A manufacturing company wanted to improve safety results. They were one of the top producers in their industry, but they were still hurting forty or fifty people every year in their operations and the CEO was very unhappy with those results. He genuinely cared about the people in the company, and personally knew many of their families. He did not want to see anyone get hurt.

He asked the safety and operations teams to collaborate on a plan to reduce injuries. They ran a company-wide survey, interviewed a bunch of people, did observations in production areas, and looked at the injury data. They decided that one part of the solution needed to be more support for frontline workers from their direct supervisor.

They asked the supervisors to spend more time on the floor talking to their teams to coach them on working safely, but they got no response from supervisors. The supervisors' managers could not figure out why the supervisors wouldn't just do what they asked them to do. The safety director had good relationships with some of the supervisors, so they all went to lunch one day. Perhaps because of their relationship, the trust they had built, and the fact they did not work for the safety director, the supervisors eventually opened up and cautiously shared that it was too much to ask them to add this task to their already overflowing plates.

Besides, what would they say if they walked around talking to people? Their team changed every day, based on the needs of the site, so they barely knew anyone on their teams. They already asked people to "be safe," what more is there to do? They knew there were some hard cases at the site who wouldn't change no matter what they did, and those were some of the best workers they had, so the supervisors just ignored the unsafe behavior from those individuals. Plus, even if they did try to correct the unsafe behavior of those individuals, the union would fight them all the way, and it was not worth the headaches.

The safety and ops team leaders did a weeklong time audit of the supervisors' day by having a staff member shadow one supervisor to record everything he did all day long. They discovered that most of the activities required the supervisor to be in the office on his computer. This meant that he could not be in the manufacturing areas talking to people unless he chose to skip part of his job. They wrote down everything the supervisor was asked to do and determined the core tasks for the job. Everything else was delegated or dropped. Almost immediately, the supervisors had more time to spend on the work floor.

The leaders made a change to the scheduling process, so that each supervisor had a set team each day. There were still occasional modifications, but this allowed supervisors to get to know the people they were being asked to coach and created a better environment for the behavior to occur.

They dealt with the complaint that supervisors did not know what to say by holding a course on effective supervisory conversations (taught by me), adding coaching and encouragement from their managers, and giving the supervisors conversation cards[15] to get to know their team. Each deck of cards contained one hundred open-ended questions they could ask their team members (e.g., "What do you like about working here?"). We wanted them to ask open-ended questions instead of closed questions (e.g., "Is everything okay?") because the former creates a dialogue, builds the relationship, and teaches the question-asker something about the person they are talking to.

In the morning, the supervisor could select a few cards and keep them on his clipboard to remind him which questions to ask throughout the day. Asking open-ended questions helped them build relationships. Within a month of doing this, a survey showed that even the most disgruntled employees said the conversations made it feel like their supervisor cared about their safety.

The safety and ops team leaders notified the workforce that this was all happening because they were serious about safety were and they did not want to see anyone get hurt. If they felt they were put in an unsafe situation while working, they were encouraged to stop the work and talk about it with their supervisor or coworkers. The leaders held skip-level meetings to ask employees how often they talked to their supervisor, what their conversations were like, and what barriers they had to working safely. Through the conversations, supervisors learned that PPE was sometimes unavailable and often uncomfortable, so they sourced new and better PPE and they started asking questions to discover barriers when they saw noncompliance.

Finally, the supervisors were given training to deliver discipline that adhered to union rules. They engaged union leaders in this training and gained their commitment to help their workers get more focused on safety and listen to their supervisor's coaching.

This may sound like a lot of effort—and it was—but this is an example of preparing the soil. When the initial request was made, supervisors didn't have the time, the skills, the relationships, or the equipment they needed to do their job. I'm sure some were also not thrilled with being asked to do yet another thing. Only once the other leaders created the right environment could the supervisors do what they had been asked to do.

Caring about safety wasn't just a talking point for leaders, and the employees knew this. The number of injuries dropped significantly and worker engagement in safety increased. They had improved the physical and psychological safety of their teams.

Summary

Aside from improving outcomes, why do we have to worry about creating the conditions for change to work? People do not like to feel they have no control over a situation or their lives, and this is especially true at work. In behavioral language, this distaste might take the form of active or passive "counter control"[16] wherein people work against your goals or more passively withdraw from the situation and fail to participate like you had hoped. Some studies have even suggested that when people work in a highly controlling and negative environment, they are more likely to steal office supplies or report inaccurate work time to exert counter control.

I cringe when I hear some leaders say they'd like to do behavioral science or OBM to someone. If you are thinking this, you might want to unpack this to discover what is making you want to make people to do something they don't want to do. Such an approach is diametrically opposed to everything I've presented in this book. Although it might work in some short-term instances, it is a poor strategy for the long term as it feels controlling and manipulative. Again, the "try this at home first" strategy applies here—how would it work at home for your partner or loved one to feel as though you were doing something to control their behavior?

The elements in this chapter set the foundation or "prepare the soil for planting." These do not make up a process in a strict sense. That is, I'm not arguing that you need to lay the groundwork before you can use the five-step Behavior Change Process to make improvements. In the real world it may be impractical to do these in sequence, and you might need to do everything you can whenever you can.

The point I hope you take away as a reader and leader is that, as you grow the relationship, trust, and communication side of your skillset, your behavioral science techniques will become more and more effective and easier to apply. Relationships and all the activities you do to build them are the fuel that will help you succeed in learning how to apply behavioral principles to managing and leading staff and teams more effectively.

Rate Yourself

Download a fillable PDF of this worksheet at
www.reachingresults.com/results-toolkit

Rate yourself and your organization or team on the topics in this
chapter. Create a plan to develop one or more of them. Clearly this
is a very subjective exercise, but there is evidence that even subjective self-reflection can be helpful, so give it a try.

1. Create a psychologically safe workplace

How would you rate your ability to create a safe space for your
team to say what is on their minds?

1	2	3	4	5
Worst				**Best**

How would you rate your department or division in creating a
safe space for people to say what is on their minds?

1	2	3	4	5
Worst				**Best**

How would you rate your organization in creating a safe space
for people to say what is on their minds?

1	2	3	4	5
Worst				**Best**

2. Recognize the importance of relationships

Do people get regular supportive and developmental coaching
from their direct supervisor?

Never	**Rarely**	**Sometimes**	**Mostly**	**Always**

Do people speak to their direct supervisor every day? Multiple
times per week? Less often?

1	2	3	4	5
Worst				**Best**

3. Strategies for building relationships

Have you done any of these:

● Create a relationship map?   **Yes / No**

How would you do this in your organization?

_____

_____

_____

If you have tried it, how could you do it better?

_____

_____

_____

● Learn about the person   **Yes / No**

How do leaders in your organization do this now?

_____

_____

_____

How could leaders in your organization do it better?

_____

_____

_____

● Use reinforcer surveys   **Yes / No**

How could you try this?

_____

_____

_____

If you're doing it now, how could you do it better?

_____

_____

_____

- Engage in planned conversations   **Yes / No**

  Is there something you could try to make this happen more reliably and more effectively?

_____

_____

_____

- Measure how your conversations are received   **Yes / No**

  How do you collect this data?

_____

_____

_____

  How often do you share it as feedback to leaders?

_____

_____

_____

- Recognize the whole person comes to work   **Yes / No**

  How do leaders demonstrate this?

_____

_____

_____

• Learn, understand, and apply the ABC model of behavior
Yes / No

How can you ensure that this is happening and being applied
to leadership and management in your organization?

_____

_____

_____

How does any of this relate to the improvement project you
selected?

_____

_____

_____

CHAPTER 9

Applying the Contents of this Book

You have made it to the end of this book, and the goal now is to apply what you have learned. This chapter will help you do that and help others around you to apply it as well. One theme of this book is that we rely too much on knowledge and awareness when trying to produce behavior change. Knowing something is different from doing it. Being aware of something does not mean we will act on it.

Therefore, if you read this book as a team or hand it to your coworkers, we can assume that it is difficult to get people to apply the five steps unless you have created an environment in which they are encouraged to do so. That is easier said than done. The same is true of any book, video, or training. There is something you can do about it though. I have spent many years working on getting change to last, and there are some things that have reliably worked. I'd like to share some of those with you in this chapter.

In some ways, spreading these skills through the organization and sustaining the improvements created are the hardest parts of all. This is a reason I am called as a consultant or facilitator. I help people learn to apply behavioral techniques and produce measurable improvements throughout their organization.

Here are some ideas for how you can sustain the positive effects created by the Behavior Change Process:

Create a sustainability plan

Decide who should be involved, what you would like them to do, and what kinds of positive consequences you can plan in for their engagement.

Bring the language into your meetings

If someone speaks in vague terms, ask them to "pinpoint that, please." Ask if they have any data when you hear them make an assumption. This is not a weapon to use against ideas you don't like but rather a way to get curious about the veracity of assumptions we hold. Test for expectations by asking coworkers what they are being asked to do in a specific situation. Promote scientific thinking.

Have a book club or hold an annual internal conference

It's not as extensive as some of the other approaches, but each can promote continuous learning. I am often called on as a speaker for internal conferences and learning events, and these are a great way to level up the skills on your teams.

Conduct leadership surveys, getting anonymous input from team members to share with their direct supervisor.

Expect the direct supervisor to respond well to the feedback and pick something to improve.

Build BSL practices into your strategic plan

A manufacturing client did this and set the expectation that all leaders were expected to use these techniques in their approach to any improvements they wanted in their departments. This is a great way to get leaders focused on the impact they have on their teams.

Measure the number of projects and amount of savings they produce

Share the data widely; promote and praise the leaders who show they are using it.

Create a group assignment to address important results

A healthcare client did this to improve handwashing through-out their centers. A manufacturing client did this to improve yield on their highest-profit products, earning them millions.

Expect all leaders to always have a personal improvement plan, focused on one of their skills they could do better. Ask for one new or continuing improvement project per quarter (or per year).

Share the project results every so often in a session where leaders give public praise for the work.

Train all your leaders in Behavioral Science for Leaders

The best effects over the past twenty-five years, in my experience, come from hiring companies who are professionals at teaching behavioral science rather than trying to do it on your own. If you can't hire a company like this, then getting the knowledge to your team in any way you can is better than nothing.

> *"You can do anything you want in life.*
> *You just can't do it all at the same time."*
>
> —Brian Chesky, CEO, Airbnb

Leadership

The five-step Behavior Change Process in this book is not "leadership," per se, but it represents some key leader behaviors:

1. Pinpoint

2. Measure

3. Agree on expectations

4. Feedback

5. Recognize improvement

Executing these five steps is a part of a leader's repertoire. Most clients I have worked with over the years want to know what other leader behaviors are needed to produce the results they want to see. Although there is no magic formula, there are many evidence-based elements of effective leadership. When faced with a very long list of behaviors that have a positive impact on team members and results, I tend to group them into three primary areas: Self-Management, Relationship Management, and Performance Management.

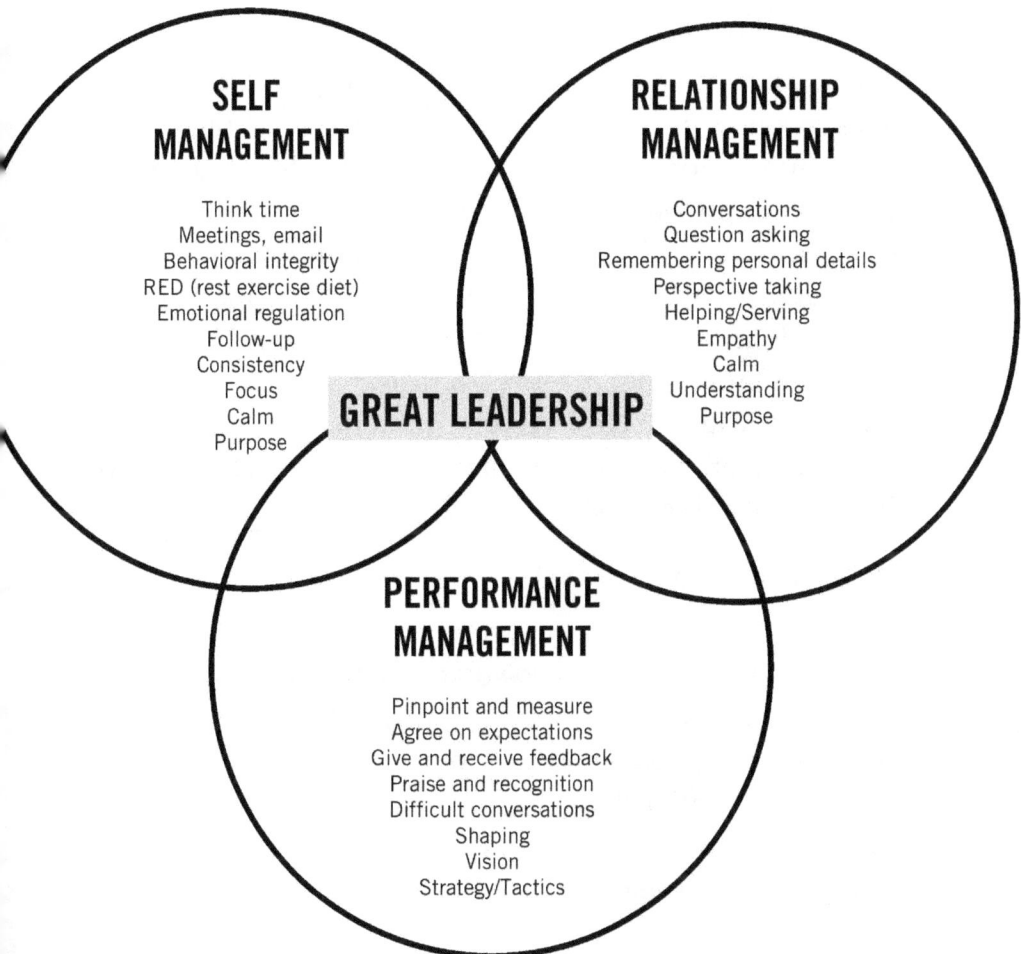

SELF MANAGEMENT

Think time
Meetings, email
Behavioral integrity
RED (rest exercise diet)
Emotional regulation
Follow-up
Consistency
Focus
Calm
Purpose

RELATIONSHIP MANAGEMENT

Conversations
Question asking
Remembering personal details
Perspective taking
Helping/Serving
Empathy
Calm
Understanding
Purpose

GREAT LEADERSHIP

PERFORMANCE MANAGEMENT

Pinpoint and measure
Agree on expectations
Give and receive feedback
Praise and recognition
Difficult conversations
Shaping
Vision
Strategy/Tactics

Each of the three areas involves many leader behaviors, and each area depends on the others, as the image shows. After coaching hundreds of leaders, I've found that these are the primary areas and behaviors that people tend to struggle with. Therefore, these have been built into my Behavioral Science for Leaders courses and my coaching. I believe these are essential elements when applying behavioral science techniques. It's beyond the scope of this book to go into great depth on these, but I will give a summary of them.

Self-management

This involves managing your own behavior as a leader. This means doing the things required to create the proper environment for your success. Doing this helps keep you calm under pressure, reduces anxiety, and gives you proper rest and diet so that you can perform at your best. Self-management means being organized, responding to email and calls in a timely manner, and managing your time, among many other things. Without proper self-management, you can't effectively influence others, consistently deliver, support organizational initiatives, or have high-quality thoughts and ideas.

Relationship Management

This is required to influence, help, support, and understand what is important to your coworkers. This involves practices such as having effective conversations, asking curious questions, listening, challenging people, and developing trusting and caring relationships. Some of these require some effort to pinpoint and measure, which is probably why they have not gotten the treatment from behavior analysts I believe they deserve.

Performance Management

The area where the five-step Behavior Change Process is found. It's the domain that we know the most about in applied behavior analysis. The performance management techniques we have at our disposal (e.g., feedback, recognition, etc.) are fantastic and effective, but we must keep in mind that they are delivered by people to other people. Techniques matter, but so do relationships (Relationship Management), and those relationships and techniques are more effective when delivered by people who can effectively manage their behavior (Self-Management) and model the correct practices.

The three areas of Self-Management, Relationship Management, and Performance Management are interrelated. All of them are important for leaders to develop in themselves and others. Mastery of the behaviors in these three areas makes everything you do in the organization more effective.

Mastery of the behaviors in these three areas makes everything you do in the organization more effective.

Deliberate Practice Helps You Improve

How do you bring out the best results?

The organizations with the best results from applying these behavioral techniques have some things in common:

They internalize the concepts

Behavioral science becomes a way of thinking that drives the operation of the organization. You start to see it in their recruitment, hiring, onboarding, training, quality, production, supervision, communication, and even their strategy. They find that they can improve their other programs with behavioral science. Programs like Lean, 6-Sigma, organizational effectiveness, large-scale implementations, and even mergers can be improved by integrating the concepts taught in this book.

They practice

Leaders keep their teams focused on making small but consistent improvements. People might start out by solving problems involving themselves, then their team, and then within departments or across functions. One organization decreased cost of service by 50% through consistently asking for improvement ideas and implementing them using behavior change strategies. Another organization saved millions by improving scheduled maintenance by 30% by measuring the critical behaviors, making the results visible (feedback), and recognizing improvements.[1]

Psychologist Anders Ericsson is famous for the 10,000 hour rule, saying you can become an expert in any area by practicing 10,000 hours or more. It is not widely known that the "practice" must include timely and specific feedback, which we learned about in chapter 6, for it to count toward the 10,000 hours! You don't need to practice for 10,000 hours to learn behavioral thinking, but some practice does help you quickly improve.

They set the expectation that it will be used

Leaders ask their teams to use behavioral approaches to solve everyday problems (e.g., running effective meetings) and, eventually, larger challenges (e.g., plant-wide maintenance shutdowns, improving billing utilization and IT implementations), and they model behavioral thinking and practices (e.g., pinpointing, feedback, recognition) on their own teams and projects. Some leaders have made behavioral science skills a prerequisite for promotion in the organization.

They recognize people for using the skills

Leaders in highly effective organizations build behavioral science skills into their performance evaluations and their everyday coaching or mentoring so that people who use the best practices also get rewarded in their review and perhaps also financially. Recognition can happen any time though, not just during performance evaluation, so when these effective leaders see something good happen, they praise it.

They continue their education

When new leaders and managers are hired, they are taught to think and act behaviorally. Existing leaders also continue their education, because as I said earlier in the book, behavioral science is a PhD degree subject. You don't have to know it all, but it helps you to improve if you keep absorbing new content, discussing it with your peers, and trying it out.

They focus on important results

This one is vital. Some leaders misinterpret the idea of using behavioral science to mean that they do a five-step project on everything. Although it is important to start small and improve your chances of success in each project to learn the skills, it is also important to take on projects that have a clear results focus.

For example, a common initial project is to start giving more praise. This is very important, but at the start it's not normally directed at the behaviors vital to a particular result. A more advanced project might be improving quality, billable hours, yield, service delivery, or even profitability. You use the same five-step Behavior Change Process, but the projects are more complex—there are more people or more behaviors involved.

In closing

Many of our challenges with people come from our misunderstanding of human behavior. There is a science that can help. This book is about how to use that science and understanding of humans to create a more effective organization.

A big part of using the tools described in this book involves having dialogue with people and asking the right questions to understand the causes of their behavior before reacting to address any concerns. The five-step Behavior Change Process, and any tools you would like to use at work, will be more effective if leaders throughout your organization can:

- Create a psychologically safe space for people to be themselves and share their best ideas
- Use strategies to create better relationships among key people
- Focus on improving and measuring the quality of their conversations with their teams
- Work to understand and practice the ABC model of behavior

I would love to see the results of your improvement projects, hear what you learned from practicing these topics, or receive any feedback you have.

Connect with me at www.reachingresults.com and www.drjohnaustin.com

NOTES

Preface

1. Bosma et al. (1997).

Chapter One

1. Not the actual name. I use pseudonyms for all the examples in this book to protect their anonymity.

2. When I was a professor, university students from my research lab and I published a number of papers demonstrating this point. See Rohn, Lutrey, & Austin (2003); Fante, Shier, & Austin (2007); Shier, Rae, & Austin (2008); and others.

3. What I call *Behavioral Science for Leaders* in this book and in practice is based in part on the science of Organizational Behavior Management (OBM). OBM is the scientific application of behavioral principles in organizational settings. One set of foundational ideas that led to the development of OBM comes from Applied Behavior Analysis. Teaching OBM and ABA is beyond the scope of this book, but the reader should know that ABA began in the 1960s and is a source of evidence-based behavioral technology that has been applied in many environments, including for people with autism and disabilities, but also in schools, for sports, in the community, for preserving the environment, for animal training and zoo animal enrichment, for training and education, and of course in organizations. Learn more about ABA at www.abainternational.org

Chapter Two

1. Just three of these models are from Daniels and Bailey (2014), where you can find a seven-step model in their *Performance Management* textbook, a six-step model in Braksick's book *Unlock Behavior, Unleash Profits* (2007), and a four-step model called DO IT (define, observe,

intervene, and test) by Geller (2001). I'm sure there are more models like these, and you should seek them out to learn more. As we will discuss in this book, the magic is not in the model but in how you apply it.

2. Download a case study of over 500 projects in a manufacturing organization at www.reachingresults.com/clients-results/, and read our peer-reviewed publications demonstrating this model in manufacturing (Gravina, King, & Austin, 2019) and in an ABA services organization (Gravina & Austin, 2018).

3. I learned how to teach a similar process from Dr. Jon Bailey at Florida State University while I was a graduate student and his graduate assistant. During those years, we self-published a book full of projects at the end of each semester called *Progress in Performance Management.*

4. We have published numerous examples of this in a variety of industries. For example, see Rohn, Austin, & Lutrey, 2003.

5. Simons, 2002.

6. Goldstein, Martin, & Cialdini, 2009.

7. Larkin & Larkin, 2007.

8. Allen & Hall, 2019.

9. A couple of key sources in this field are *Mindfulness and Acceptance at Work* (Hayes, Bond, Barnes-Holmes, & Austin, 2013) and *A Liberated Mind* (Hayes, 2019).

Chapter Three

1. Johnson & Street (2014).

2. Daniels & Bailey (2014).

3. Gravina & Austin (2018).

4. Komaki (1998).

5. Alvero, Bucklin, & Austin (2001); Sleiman et al. (2020).

6. Laraway (2022).

Chapter Four

1. Losada & Heaphy (2004).

2. Shier, Rae, & Austin (2008).

3. Olson & Austin (2001).

4. Richman, Riordan, Pyles, & Bailey (1988).

5. Dean, Malott, & Fulton (1983).

6. Browder, Liberty, Heller, & D'Huyvetters (1986).

7. Whelan, Mahoney, & Meyers (1991).

8. Burgio, Whitman, & Reid (1983).

9. Moinat & Snortum (1976).

Chapter Five

1. Schaffer (1991, March 1).

2. Schaffer (2010).

3. Gravina, Nastasi, & Austin (2021).

4. Carr et al. (2013).

5. Martinez-Onstott, Wilder, & Sigurdsson (2016).

6. Hodges, Villacorta, Wilder, Ertel, & Luong (2020).

7. Lokhorst, Werner, Staats, van Dijk, & Gale (2013).

8. Oncken & Wass (1990).

9. Larkin & Larkin (2007).

10. See his video on our Youtube channel: www.youtube.com/reachingresults

11. Olson, Schmidt, Winkler, & Wipfli (2011).

Chapter Six

1. We published a study on this project: Austin, Kessler, Riccobono, & Bailey, 1996.

2. Sleiman et al. (2020).

3. Sleiman et al. (2020).

4. Johnson (2013).

5. Larkin & Larkin (2007).

6. Zenger & Folkman (2013).

7. Zenger & Folkman (2014).

8. Matey, Sleiman, Nastasi, Richard, & Gravina (2021).

9. Laraway (2022).

10. Zenger & Folkman (2013).

11. Thanks to Dr. Nicole Gravina for sharing this example!

12. Goldsmith (2015, October 29).

13. Ehrlich, Nosik, Carr, & Wine (2020).

14. Renninger (2020, February 10).

15. Scott (2020).

16. Patterson, Grenny, McMillan, & Switzler (2002).

17. Fournies (1999).

Chapter Seven

1. If you want to dive deeper into the topic of using reinforcement, recognition, and praise at work, you should read Daniels and Bailey (2014). The list below is pulled from my experience, their book, and other sources too.

2. Losada & Heaphy (2004).

3. Daniels (2009).

4. Cook et al. (2017).

5. Losada & Heaphy (2004).

6. Gottman, Coan, Carrere, & Swanson (1998).

7. Schulz & Wilder (2022).

8. Clear (2018).

9. If you'd like to learn more about consequence types, see Cooper, Heron, & Heward (2007) or Daniels & Bailey (2014).

10. Ferster & Skinner (1957) wrote the book on this topic and you should read it if you really want to go in depth on this topic; however, Daniels & Bailey (2014) cover it in a practical way for work applications if you would like something more accessible to read.

11. One example is Abernathy's *The Sin of Wages* (1996).

Chapter Eight

1. Curry et al. (2019).

2. Edmonson (2018).

3. Duhigg (2016, February 25).

4. Patterson et al. (2002).

5. Edmonson (2018).

6. Clark (2020).

7. Howard Lees, Hollin Consulting.

8. Ascend behavior partners: Hiring in a tight labor market (n.d.).

9. Daniels & Bailey (2014).

10. Aron et al. (1997).

11. See the backstory here: https://www.mindbodygreen.com/articles/36-questions-to-fall-in-love

12. Thanks to Kim Scott's *Radical Candor* for that one!

13. Semler (1995).

14. Called *task clarification* by Anderson et al. (1988).

15. Available through Sodak.co.uk at https://sodak.co.uk/shop/100-conversations-to-reduce-risk/

16. Counter control is a term defined by B.F. Skinner in 1953 to denote the practice opposing or resisting an intervention imposed by others. It can take an active (e.g., direct verbal or physical opposition) or passive form (e.g., simply not responding to behavior change attempts). A form of resistance to change, avoiding counter control is a great reason to engage the individuals whose behavior is being pinpointed for change.

Chapter Nine

1. Unscheduled maintenance in manufacturing operations can be as much as four times more costly than scheduled maintenance.

REFERENCES

Abernathy, W. B. (1996). *The Sin of Wages: Where the Conventional Pay System has Led Us and How.* Performance Management Publications.

Allen, D., & Hall, B. (2019). *The Getting Things Done Workbook: 10 Moves to Stress-Free Productivity.* Penguin.

Alvero, A. M., Bucklin, B. R., & Austin, J. (2001). An objective review of the effectiveness and essential characteristics of performance feedback in organizational settings. *Journal of Organizational Behavior Management, 21*(1), 3–29. DOI:10.1300/j075v21n01_02

Anderson, Crowell, Hantula, Siroky (1988). Task Clarification and Individual Performance Posting for Improving Cleaning in a Student-Managed University Bar *Journal of Organizational Behavior Management, 9*(2),73–90. DOI:10.1300/J075v09n02_06

Aron, A., Melinat, E., Aron, E. N., Vallone, R. D., & Bator, R. J. (1997). The experimental generation of interpersonal closeness: A procedure and some preliminary findings. *Personality & Social Psychology Bulletin, 23*(4), 363–377. https://doi.org/10.1177/0146167297234003

Ascend behavior partners: Hiring in a tight labor market. (n.d.). Stanford Graduate School of Business. Retrieved January 18, 2023, from https://www.gsb.stanford.edu/faculty-research/case-studies/ascend-behavior-partners-hiring-tight-labor-market

Austin, J., Kessler, M. L., Riccobono, J. E., & Bailey, J. S. (1996). Using feedback and reinforcement to improve the performance and safety of a roofing crew. *Journal of Organizational Behavior Management, 16*(2), 49–75.

Bosma, H., Marmot, M. G., Hemingway, H., Nicholson, A. C., Brunner, E., & Stansfeld, S. A. (1997). Low job control and risk of coronary heart disease in Whitehall II (prospective cohort) study. *Bmj, 314*(7080), 558.

Browder, D. M., Liberty, K., Heller, M., & D'Huyvetters, K. K. (1986). Self-management by teachers: Improving instructional decision-making. *Professional School Psychology, 1* (3), 165–175.

Burgio, L. D., Whitman, T. L., & Reid, D. H. (1983). A participative management approach for improving direct-care staff performance in an institutional setting. *Journal of Applied Behavior Analysis, 16*, 37–53.

Braksick, L. W. (2007). *Unlock behavior, unleash profits: Developing leadership behavior that drives profitability in your organization* (2nd ed.). McGraw-Hill Education.

Carr, J. E., Wilder, D. A., Majdalany, L., Mathisen, D., & Strain, L. A. (2013). An assessment-based solution to a human-service employee performance problem. *Behavior Analysis in Practice, 6*(1), 16–32. doi:10.1007/bf03391789

Clark, T. R. (2020). *The 4 stages of psychological safety: Defining the path to inclusion and innovation.* Berrett-Koehler Publishers.

Cooper, J., Heron, T., & Heward, W., (2007). *Applied behavior analysis.* (2nd ed.) Pearson.

Clear, J. (2018). *Atomic habits: Tiny changes, remarkable results: An easy and proven way to build good habits & break bad ones.* Avery.

Cook, C. R., Grady, E. A., Long, A. C., Renshaw, T., Codding, R. S., Fiat, A., & Larson, M. (2017). Evaluating the Impact of Increasing General Education Teachers' Ratio of Positive-to-Negative Interactions on Students' Classroom Behavior. *Journal of Positive Behavior Interventions, 19*(2), 67–77. https://doi.org/10.1177/1098300716679137

Cooper, J. O., Heward, W. L., Heron, T. E. (2020). *Applied Behavior Analysis.* Pearson.

Curry, S. M., Gravina, N. E., Sleiman, A. A., & Richard, E. (2019). The effects of engaging in rapport-building behaviors on productivity and discretionary effort. *Journal of Organizational Behavior Management, 39*(3–4), 213–226.

Daniels, A. C. (2009). *Oops! 13 management practices that waste time and money (and what to do instead).* Performance Management Publications.

Daniels, A. C., & Bailey, J. S. (2014). *Performance Management.* Performance Management Publications.

Dean, M. R., Malott, R. W., & Fulton, B. J. (1983). The effects of self-management training on academic performance. *Teaching of Psychology, 10* (2), 77–81.

Duhigg, C. (2016, February 25). What Google learned from its quest to build the perfect team. *The New York Times.* https://www.nytimes.com/2016/02/28/magazine/what-google-learned-from-its-quest-to-build-the-perfect-team.html

Edmondson, A. C. (2018). *The Fearless Organization.* John Wiley & Sons.

Ehrlich, R. J., Nosik, M. R., Carr, J. E., & Wine, B. (2020). Teaching employees how to receive feedback: A preliminary investigation. *Journal of Organizational Behavior Management, 40*(1–2), 19–29.

Fante, R., Shier, L., & Austin, J. (2007). Utilizing task clarification and self-monitoring to increase food temperature checks among restaurant staff. *Journal of Foodservice Business Research, 9*(2–3), 67–88.

Ferster, C. B. (n.d.). *Schedules of Reinforcement.* (n.p.): B. F. Skinner Foundation.

Fournies, F. F. (1999). *Coaching for Improved Work Performance.* (Revised edition). McGraw Hill.

Geller, E. S. (2001). Behavior-based safety in industry: Realizing the large-scale potential of psychology to promote human welfare. *Applied and Preventive Psychology, 10*(2), 87–105.

Gottman J. M., Coan J., Carrere S., & Swanson C. (1998). Predicting marital happiness and stability from newlywed interactions. *Journal of Marriage and the Family, 60*, 5–22.

Goldsmith, M. (2015, October 29). Try feedforward instead of feedback. https://www.marshallgoldsmith.com/articles/try-feedforward-instead-feedback/

Goldstein, N. J., Martin, S. J., & Cialdini, R. (2009). *Yes!: 50 Scientifically proven ways to be persuasive.* Simon & Schuster.

Gravina, N., & Austin, J. (2018). An evaluation of the consultant workshop model in a human service setting. *Journal of Organizational Behavior Management, 38*(2–3), 244–257.

Gravina, N. E., King, A., & Austin, J. (2019). Training leaders to apply behavioral concepts to improve safety. *Safety science, 112*, 66–70.

Gravina, N., Nastasi, J., & Austin, J. (2021). Assessment of employee performance. *Journal of Organizational Behavior Management, 41*(2), 124–149.

Hayes, S. (2019). *A Liberated Mind: The essential guide to ACT.* Vermilion.

Hayes, S. C., Bond, F. W., Barnes-Holmes, D., & Austin, J. (Eds.). (2006). Acceptance and mindfulness at work: Applying acceptance and commitment therapy and relational frame theory to organizational behavior management. Routledge.

Hodges, A. C., Villacorta, J., Wilder, D. A., Ertel, H., & Luong, N. (2020). Assessment and improvement of parent training: An evaluation of the Performance Diagnostic Checklist–Parent. *Behavioral Development Bulletin, 25*(1), 1–16. https://doi.org/10.1037/bdb0000092

Komaki, J. L. (1998*). Leadership from an Operant Perspective.* Routledge.

Johnson, D. A. (2013). A component analysis of the impact of evaluative and objective feedback on performance. *Journal of Organizational Behavior Management, 33*, 89–103. doi:10.1080/01608061.2013.785879

Johnson, K., & Street, E. M. (2014). Precision teaching: The legacy of Ogden Lindsley. In F. K. McSweeney & E. S. Murphy (Eds.), *The Wiley Blackwell handbook of operant and classical conditioning* (pp. 581–609). Wiley Blackwell. https://doi.org/10.1002/9781118468135.ch23

Laraway, R. (2022). *When They Win, You Win: Being a Great Manager Is Simpler Than You Think.* St. Martin's Publishing Group.

Larkin, T. J., & Larkin, S. (2007). You know safety but admit it . . . you don't know communication. Larkin Communication Consulting.

Lokhorst, A. M., Werner, C., Staats, H., van Dijk, E., & Gale, J. L. (2013). Commitment and Behavior Change: A Meta-Analysis and Critical Review of Commitment-Making Strategies in Environmental Research. *Environment and Behavior, 45*(1), 3–34. https://doi.org/10.1177/0013916511411477

Losada, M., & Heaphy, E. (2004). The role of positivity and connectivity in the performance of business teams: A nonlinear dynamics model. *American Behavioral Scientist, 47*(6), 740–765.

Martinez-Onstott, B., Wilder, D., & Sigurdsson, S. (2016). Identifying the variables contributing to at-risk performance: Initial evaluation of the performance diagnostic checklist–safety (PDC-safety). *Journal of Organizational Behavior Management, 36*(1), 80–93. https://doi.org/10.1080/01608061.2016.1152209

Matey, N., Sleiman, A., Nastasi, J., Richard, E., & Gravina, N. (2021). Varying reactions to feedback and their effects on observer accuracy and feedback omission. *Journal of Applied Behavior Analysis, 54*(3), 1188–1198.

Moinat, S., & Snortum, J. R. (1976). Self-management of personal habits by female drug addicts: A feasibility study. *Criminal Justice & Behavior, 3* (1), 29–40.

Olson, R., & Austin, J. (2001). Behavior-Based Safety and Working Alone: The Effects of a Self-Monitoring Package on the Safe Performance of Bus Operators. *Journal of Organizational Behavior Management* (3) 5–43.

Olson, R., Schmidt, S., Winkler, C., & Wipfli, B. (2011). The effects of target behavior choice and self-management skills training on compliance with behavioral self-monitoring. *American Journal of Health Promotion: AJHP, 25*(5), 319–324. https://doi.org/10.4278/ajhp.090421-quan-143

Oncken Jr, W., & Wass, D. L. (1990). Management time: who's got the monkey? *Journal of Nursing Administration, 20*(12), 6–9.

Patterson, K., Grenny, J., McMillan, R., & Switzler, A. (2002). *Crucial conversations: Tools for talking when stakes are high.* McGraw Hill.

Renninger, L. (2020, February 10). *LeeAnn Renninger: The secret to giving great feedback.*

Richman, G. S., Riordan, M. R., Reiss, M. L., Pyles, D. A., & Bailey, J. S. (1988). The effects of self-monitoring and supervisor feedback on staff performance in a residential setting. *Journal of Applied Behavior Analysis, 21*(4), 401–409. https://doi.org/10.1901/jaba.1988.21-401

Rohn, D., Austin, J., & Lutrey, S. M. (2003). Using feedback and performance accountability to decrease cash register shortages. *Journal of Organizational Behavior Management, 22*(1), 33–46.

Schaffer, R. H. (1991, March 1). Demand better results—and get them. *Harvard Business Review.* https://hbr.org/1991/03/demand-better-results-and-get-them

Schaffer, R. H. (2010). Four mistakes leaders keep making. *Harvard Business Review, 88*(9), 86–91, 126. https://hbr.org/2010/09/four-mistakes-leaders-keep-making

Schulz, A., & Wilder, D. A. (2022). The Use of Task Clarification and Self-Monitoring to Increase Affirmative to Constructive Feedback Ratios in Supervisory Relationships. *Journal of Organizational Behavior Management, 42*(3), 244–254.

Scott, K. (2020). *Radical candor: Be a kick-ass boss without losing your humanity.* St. Martin's Griffin.

Semler, R. (1993). *Maverick: The Success Story behind the World's Most Unusual Workplace.* Warner Books.

Shier, L., Rae, C., & Austin, J. (2008). Using Task Clarification, Checklists and Performance Feedback to Improve the Appearance of a Grocery Store. *Performance Improvement Quarterly, 16*(2), 26–40. https://doi.org/10.1111/j.1937-8327.2003.tb00277

Skinner, B. F. (1953). *Science and Human Behavior.* Macmillan.

Simons, T. (2002). Behavioral integrity: the perceived alignment between managers' words and deeds as a research focus. *Organization Science, 13*, 18–35.

Sleiman, A. A., Sigurjonsdottir, S., Elnes, A., Gage, N. A., & Gravina, N. E. (2020). A quantitative review of performance feedback in organizational settings (1998–2018). *Journal of Organizational Behavior Management, 40*(3–4), 303–332. https://doi.org/10.1080/01608061.2020.1823300

Whelan, J., Mahoney, M. J., & Meyers, A. W. (1991). Performance enhancement in sport: A cognitive behavioral domain. *Behavior Therapy, 22* (3), 307–327.

Zenger, J., & Folkman, J. (2013). Nice or tough: Which approach engages employees most. *Harvard Business Review.*

Zenger, J., & Folkman, J. (2014). Your employees want the negative feedback you hate to give. *Harvard Business Review.*

ACKNOWLEDGMENTS

The support I received from family, friends, clients, and colleagues is what made this book possible (plus setting a challenging deadline!).

A master storyteller for leaders, my wife, Allison, spent hours poring over early drafts of structure and story with incisive clarity to help me say what I wanted to say. My son Michael helped me with his keen eye for design. My friends Nicole Gravina and Bob Cummins read multiple versions and gave me insightful and rapid feedback.

Multiple colleagues and clients who are all incredibly busy took the time to read an early version of this book and give me feedback, including: Ivy Chong, Paulie Gavoni, Bob George, Brian Hanlon, Kevin Kirk, Linda LeBlanc, Stuart Mason, Niall McConville, Jonathan Mueller, Tim Rosbrook, Tyra Sellers, and Jim Carr. Thanks to Mike O'Shaughnessy, CEO of Revere Copper, for schooling me on "How CEOs read books." Best class I've taken in quite a while! Special thanks to Steve East, Chairman of CSM Group, for his feedback, loyalty, and for teaching me so much over the years.

The ACES+ Mastermind Group, along with Danny Iny and Bhoomi Pathak, gave me lots of developmental feedback, accountability, and praise along the way. Lisa Bloom, my ACES coach, is a master storyteller and wordsmith and generously lent all her strengths, all the time. Julie Haase, Jennifer Bright, Ally Machate, and the team at The Writer's Ally for professionally managing all of the publishing process and keeping me on time.

I learned this all from hundreds of clients and students

in nineteen countries, but first I learned it from my teachers. Vic Corbin, my high school Spanish teacher who was a behavior analyst but probably didn't know it; Dr. D. Chris Anderson, my first professor of behavior analysis; and Dr. Jon Bailey, my doctoral mentor. The teaching, coaching, and support from Dr. E. Scott Geller, Dr. Aubrey Daniels, Dr. Beth Sulzer-Azaroff, Dr. Terry McSween, Dr. Judy Agnew, Howard Lees, Dr. Tim Ludwig, and Dr. Tom Krause, plus many others, had a profound influence on my thinking.

ABOUT THE AUTHOR

Dr. John Austin is an internationally recognized expert in human performance. He is CEO of Reaching Results, where he teaches leaders to create more effective work environments. Dr. Austin was also a professor of psychology at Western Michigan University. He has consulted with organizations for 30 years to improve productivity and safety.

John and his teams have been instrumental in delivering over 10,000 work improvement, quality, and safety projects that have generated millions of dollars in improvements to businesses. They have coached over 350 senior leaders from many companies and 19 countries to help them improve business performance.

In the area of improving human performance John has published nearly 100 articles and chapters, delivered hundreds of presentations at regional, national, and international conferences and business meetings, and has published three books, *Organizational Change, Handbook of Applied Behavior Analysis, and Mindfulness at Work.*

John coaches leaders; teaches courses on behavioral leadership, difficult conversations, and safety leadership; and is an event speaker on these topics.

ADDITIONAL RESOURCES TO SUPPORT YOU!

Download the *RESULTS* Toolkit and your FREE AUDIOBOOK

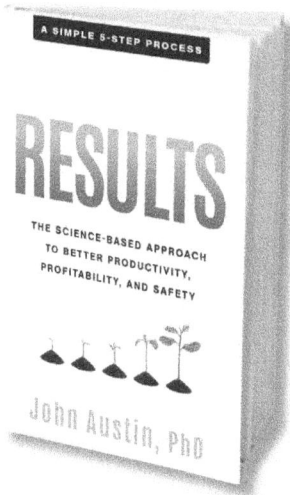

A SIMPLE 5-STEP PROCESS

RESULTS

THE SCIENCE-BASED APPROACH TO BETTER PRODUCTIVITY, PROFITABILITY, AND SAFETY

John Austin, PhD

READ THIS FIRST

Just to say thank you for reading my book, I want to share the *RESULTS* Toolkit, at no cost.

It's my gift to you.

GO TO:

www.reachingresults.com/ results-toolkit